Every so often an opportun[...] master; a person who not on[...] has p[...] reached a high level of success, but knows how to teach the 'how-to' just as effectively to others. If you want to know why winners win, simply read this amazing book. On the other hand, if you want to be one of those winners, read the book and immediately begin to apply the knowledge and wisdom the author has so generously shared. If you could only read one book on success and it would have to be enough, this book would qualify. Oh, and despite it being mostly geared to real estate, the principles Gary teaches will work for any entrepreneur; any professional. FANTASTIC!

— **Bob Burg**, co-author of *The Go-Giver*

Gary is well qualified to write a book on winning. I have seen him go from deep financial difficulties to prosperity. I have known him in tough times and good times. I have seen him build a training company that offers ethical training that works. I trust Gary's advice.

Personally, I believe we are on this 'Trip Earth' to help others. Gary had that all figured out when I met him; it is the key to our friendship! He is very aware that when he wins, everyone else in his circle does too, and Gary has helped countless people to succeed while on his own success path. Although much of his background has been in real estate, *Why Winners Win* is relevant to all industries and professions.

— **Bill Nasby**, sales trainer, international speaker, and developer of *Your Path to Deliberate Creation* and *Doors to Success*

Gary Pittard's training has helped me in two ways. First, it has had a great influence on my character and helped me become the person I am today. Second, Gary's advice gave my career direction, teaching me in logical sequences about the role of a salesperson and how to handle the mental challenges we face every day.

Through Gary I learned to set goals, which enabled me as a single mother to provide a better life for myself and my family. I developed courage to do those important, but sometimes difficult, tasks and I learned to persist and became more confident — critical attributes for success.

— **Sandy Rogers**, salesperson,
Marsellos Pike Real Estate, Morayfield Qld

I have known Gary Pittard for over 10 years and he has been instrumental in my skill development, training ability and the successes I have achieved whilst operating in real estate, and more recently running my own agency.

It is my genuine belief that his material is second to none, and that following the plans and programs he has in place will all but guarantee your success in real estate.

— **Adam Horth**, Principal, Johnson Real Estate,
Ipswich Qld

Gary Pittard is Australia's #1 expert on success in real estate. In *Why Winners Win*, Gary has combined three decades of experience, discipline and wisdom with contemporary thinking and practical, cutting-edge strategies. *Why Winners Win* is a blueprint for success. Schedule a day to read it, because once you pick it up you won't be able to put it down!

— **Mark McKeon**, author of *Every Day Counts*
and *Work a Little Less, Live a Little More*

Gary is passionate about business improvement. I worked with him to revamp his organisation's people strategies and it was unusual to find someone so open and willing to change. An early adopter of innovative practices, he uses the latest technology such as podcasts, webinars and Pittard TV to continually transform his business. Gary pursues excellence with a single-mindedness that is refreshing in an era when many leaders are still resistant to change.

— **Mandy Johnson**, author of *Winning the War for Talent*

If anyone knows about winning in a sales situation, it's Gary Pittard.

If you're serious about your sales career, this book is for you. It's free of hype and full of practical, tried and true tips to help you also become a winner. It will help you better understand your clients' needs and wants in order to better serve them.

Unlike some salespeople, Gary doesn't spout meaningless platitudes but generously and genuinely shares strategies and information that have helped him — and others he has coached — to succeed.

For anyone in real estate sales, this book is absolutely essential; I believe it is also useful for any sales environment. We're all in 'Sales' to some degree or other, and I particularly liked the segments on affirmations, persistence, quality and lifelong learning.

Gary walks the talk. He's the real deal with real knowledge for real estate selling success. Gary is indeed a winner in my book.

— **Catherine DeVrye**, former Australian Executive
Woman of the Year and #1 best-selling author of
Good Service is Good Business, *Hope as My Compass*,
Hope Happens, *Hot Lemon and Honey*
and four other titles

Gary is a rare individual. He is one of the 2 per cent club: a special club of people who actually get things done. While others wonder what they should do next, Gary does it! A quiet achiever, he personifies the saying that 'Leaders walk softly and make a big impact'. His work has inspired successful people both inside and outside the real estate industry to achieve success both professionally and personally.

— **Matt Church**, founder of Thought Leaders Global,
author of *Amplifiers* and seven other national
bestsellers on leadership

There are different types of people who work in high performance. Some people have been in the trenches and done it themselves, some people have coached others to be successful, while some have studied how people become successful. It is rare to have someone who has done all three. Gary is one of those people. He brings a unique perspective to high performance. To be the best we have to learn from the best. Gary is that person!

— **Dr Adam Fraser**, human performance researcher and author of *The Third Space*

Drawing on decades of accumulated wisdom and study, Gary Pittard shows the way to transform your sales 'job' into a distinguished career, filled with honour, heart and happiness. Under his guidance, you will learn how to establish high standards and focus a high degree of effort. The profit and wealth will follow.

This is not just a book about sales, but a book about success in life. If you are not in sales, when you read this book you'll wish you were.

— **John Kralik**, author of *A Simple Act of Gratitude (365 Thank Yous)*

I've known and worked with Gary Pittard since 2009. He is genuinely interested in improving the lives and income of the people he trains. He operates with integrity and follows through on his promises. He knows the business and delivers methods that will create winners.

— **David Knox**, international speaker, producer of online real estate video training

WHY WINNERS WIN

WHY WINNERS WIN

What it Takes to be Successful in Business and Life

GARY PITTARD

WILEY

First published in 2016 by John Wiley & Sons Australia, Ltd
42 McDougall St, Milton Qld 4064
Office also in Melbourne

Typeset in 11/13 Palatino LT Std

© Pittard Training Group Pty Ltd 2016

The moral rights of the author have been asserted

National Library of Australia Cataloguing-in-Publication data:

Creator:	Pittard, Gary, author.
Title:	Why Winners Win: what it takes to be successful in business and life / Gary Pittard.
ISBN:	9780730334163 (pbk.)
	9780730334170 (ebook)
Notes:	Includes index.
Subjects:	Success.
	Conduct of life.
	Success in business.
	Self-actualization (Psychology)
Dewey Number:	158.1

Cover design by Wiley
Cover images: head: © feelplus/Shutterstock;
brain: © NotionPic/Shutterstock

10 9 8 7 6 5 4 3 2 1

Disclaimer
The material in this publication is of the nature of general comment only, and does not represent professional advice. It is not intended to provide specific guidance for particular circumstances and it should not be relied on as the basis for any decision to take action or not take action on any matter which it covers. Readers should obtain professional advice where appropriate, before making any such decision. To the maximum extent permitted by law, the author and publisher disclaim all responsibility and liability to any person, arising directly or indirectly from any person taking or not taking action based on the information in this publication.

For my girl, Kez

CONTENTS

ABOUT THE AUTHOR

Gary Pittard is the managing director of Australia's leading real estate training and development organisation, Pittard. His sales career began in the Australian office of the global business machines and copier company Nashua.

Pittard has been servicing agents in Australia, New Zealand and Asia Pacific for more than a decade. On average, Pittard member agencies earn greater profits and experience greater levels of success than average agents. Pittard revolutionised real estate training with the development of iTrain, a digital real estate training streaming service, and Pittard TV, a live online broadcast network for real estate professionals around the world.

With more than 30 years' experience working with the best sales and leadership minds in the world, Gary has developed an acute awareness of the subtleties of human communication and influence, and the need for constant innovation and reinvention to stay relevant in rapidly changing markets.

Web: pittard.com.au
Email: info@pittard.com.au
Twitter: @garypittard
LinkedIn: linkedin.com/in/garypittard

ACKNOWLEDGEMENTS

A recurring theme throughout *Why Winners Win* is that nobody succeeds alone. The right people in both our business and personal lives not only make the difference between success and failure, but also they greatly affect our happiness and enjoyment of life. I would like to acknowledge those who contribute, and who have contributed, to any success we enjoy.

To my family: my wife Kerry (Kez), daughter Jasmin, son Jesse, their partners Adam King and Martine Zacka, our grandchildren Zachary, Bronte, Layla and Liam, and our unofficially adopted sons Patrick Casey and Thuso Lekwape. What is success without love of family? To me, it's failure of the worst kind. Life is lovely with you in it.

To the Pittard team: Michael Johnston, Ninette Maddrell, Ian Eldershaw, Martyn Jeffs, Phil Lynch, Ben Harvey, Daniel Cao, Daniel Matheson, Melanie Kikoudis and Gerald Crough. I shudder to think where we would be without you.

To the 'extended' Pittard team: Andrew and Bev Trim, Adam Horth, Jeff Cannon, Chris Pisani, Peter Tran, Samantha Peterffy, Anthony Cordato, Michael Field, Hollie Azzopardi, Kiara Bandiera, Allen and Racheal Larkin and Gihan Perera. Thank you for your friendship and sound advice, and for all of the good things you do for us.

To the late Bruce Clingan: you were the one who got me into Sales, after I returned from living overseas and was undecided about my career direction. Like all good salespeople, you made the decision for me, and then made a telephone call that was to put me on a path that I love, one that I have been on ever since. You were a champion.

Thanks to Paul Jelfs for giving me an opportunity and for your guidance in the early years of my career. Your first lesson was to tell me that a salesperson who will not prospect every day for new business is nothing but an order taker—a lesson I still teach today.

Thanks to Bill Smith and Ross Hall for all the great advice and inspiration you gave me when I first started in Sales. You taught me lessons I'll never forget, the number one being that winners care about helping others.

To Steve Lowry and Michael Simpson, who were fledgling salespeople being led by a fledgling sales manager. We met at the beginning of our careers and I admire the men and businesspeople you have become. To George Georgiou, who joined our sales training sessions in those early days, already a winner: you took the opportunity to learn more. The three of you were the beginning of my love of leadership.

Great leaders speak volumes by their actions and Ray Iacono was no exception. You became CEO while I was a sales manager trying to get a new department off the ground. I admired and respected you because you didn't spout platitudes about character and ethics: by your actions you demonstrated these characteristics, and more, every day. I learned a lot about leadership by being around you. You were fair, competent, loyal and true to your word; you cared for your people and were fun to be around. Your integrity was obvious, to work with you a privilege.

Over the years, many people have presented for Pittard, either live, on Pittard TV, or in audio programs, or have contributed in an advisory capacity behind the scenes. You have generously shared your experience and wisdom and have helped our programs to continuously improve. I cannot name you all, but these people are representative of the beautiful people that have been of great assistance to us: Andrew Trim, Adam Horth, Adam McMahon, Frank Pike, Peter O'Malley, Sandy Rogers, Michael Meakin, Steve Harris, Paul Kounnas, Chris Martin, Arthur Conias, Christina Guidotti, Catherine Ongarello, Cate Killiner, Kelvin Winnie, Adam Smith, Kay Niepold, Graham Lester, Maggie Dixon-Lester, Steve Aitken, Mark McKeon, Kevin Howlett, Nathan Brett, Gihan Perera, Bob Burg, David Knox, Bill Nasby, Dr Denis Waitley, Matt Church, Catherine DeVrye, John Kralik, Dr Adam Fraser, Mandy Johnson, Richard Flint, Margaret Lomas, Wayne Bennett, Dave Tidbold, Paul Foster, Mick Flynn, Allison Mooney, Dan Collins, and the late Peter Lees and Chas Heath. We appreciate the gift of real-world feedback from the field from great leaders, businesspeople, authors, speakers and salespeople.

When working in South-East Asia, I was privileged to meet the founders and directors of Singapore Accredited Estate Agents (SAEA): Dennis Tay, Tay Kah Poh and Peter Koh. The better I get to know you, the more I appreciate your concern for the betterment of the Singapore real estate industry. Thank you for your hospitality when I present in Singapore—the industry is lucky to have you, as am I.

To Pittard clients—members of our Leaders Circle and Winners Circle. You continue to make me proud of the results you achieve and the service you offer your clients. Our company wouldn't exist without you. Thank you for being a major part of our lives.

To my friend the late Bede Donovan and all friends of Bill Wilson. You know who you are and what your fellowship has done for me, and for my family. Keep coming back.

And finally, to my friend Dr Denis Waitley. Thank you for the generous words in your foreword, but more for the lessons you have taught me over the years. Yours was one of the first books on leadership that I ever read and we were honoured to have you present a Leadership Conference for our company. You walk your talk.

FOREWORD BY DR DENIS WAITLEY

Having devoted my life's work to studying winners in every walk of life, from Apollo astronauts to world-class athletes, from top executives of multinational corporations, to youth groups and young entrepreneurs, I consider it a privilege to offer a few opening comments about Gary Pittard's new book, *Why Winners Win*.

It has been said, with timeless wisdom, 'The greatest teachers are themselves the greatest students,' and I can say emphatically that Gary Pittard has studied 'winners' all his adult life. He is just as curious, inspired and eager to continue growing as a student of life-management attitudes and habits today as he was when he first began his upward journey to enlightenment. As with each of us, Gary was not necessarily born to win. He was born with the equal right to invest in his potential to become a winner by choice, rather than by chance. If winning in life was based on luck, Las Vegas and Macao would be ghost towns. Winning, other than the lottery, is based on universal principles that time, technology and circumstance cannot alter.

There are several major differences that make this book so relevant and special. First, although it deals with winning in the real estate industry, with a banquet of hands-on examples, *Why Winners Win* is just as applicable to every industry, leadership position, sales situation, and personal development program for individuals and family members. Another major difference is that, while quoting many icons in business and the personal growth fields, Gary does not merely recycle what he has learned by reading and studying their work, as well as attending their keynotes and workshops—he has lived his own success journey after decades of trial and error. He has earned his reputation as one of the premier sales and sales leadership experts in Australia, and I believe his book will gain global recognition as the 'winning by example' manual.

A noteworthy difference that Gary's book provides is that he structures the critical qualities of a winner in their natural progression: attitude, knowledge, skill and competent action. Attitude certainly is the primary key to our lock on the door leading to success. The right attitude opens up the treasure chest of knowledge and skills (habits) development. While many books talk about the Law of Attraction, *Why Winners Win* gives us, the readers, the most important ingredient of all: Competent Action. Winners are busy 'doing' while the rest of the population keeps 'stewing'.

I consider Gary Pittard a colleague worth emulating and a lifelong friend. If you internalise the concepts within, this book can change your life.

Dr Denis Waitley, author of *The Psychology of Winning*

INTRODUCTION

Why Winners Win shows what it takes to be successful in *any* field. It is not just for businesspeople, leaders, managers and salespeople — if you want to succeed in any endeavour, this book can help you. It is as much about success in life as it is about success in business. The two, in my opinion, are inextricably linked.

Although my work over the past two decades has focused on training real estate business owners and salespeople, before that I was in sales and sales management in the office equipment industry, and before that I worked in the hospitality industry (hotels).

So, while many of the examples I use concern real estate sales, others relate to office equipment sales and the hotel industry. Still other examples are drawn from people I have met during my life, many of whom were not businesspeople, and from books and seminars I have attended over the past three decades.

Winners are everywhere you look; unfortunately, so too are people who have chosen a different path. I learn from everyone. I recommend you do too.

It can be too easy to look at an example and say to yourself, 'This doesn't apply to me.' Perhaps the example involves someone who is not in the same field as you, but this does not mean you cannot draw parallels and learn. 'This doesn't apply to me' shuts out any possibility of learning important lessons that could change your life.

Throughout my career I have always sought winners and gone to great lengths to learn from the best. I did this before I entered Sales and Sales management, and it is a practice I continue to this day.

Why Winners Win is a distillation of lessons from my lifetime of learning. Whether you are in customer service, Sales, leadership or management, or are a salaried employee, a stay-at-home parent or just starting your working life, this book has much to offer you.

A golden opportunity

Sandy Rogers is now a high-income producer at Marsellos Pike Real Estate in Morayfield, Queensland, but her rise to the top wasn't easy.

Sandy started in the real estate business as a single mother with a young son. She has now been in the industry for about 18 years, commencing as a receptionist on $28 000 per annum, later moving into property management.

Observing the company's salespeople in action, Sandy often thought, 'I can do that.' The company gave her the opportunity to go into Sales; she put her head down, worked hard, set goals and started to forge herself a great career.

She looked after her money carefully and at one stage was able to take her family on an extended trip to Malta.

She was very gracious in thanking us for her success, but I pointed out it was really all her own doing by coming to our training programs and implementing what she had learned.

When she opened a seminar for us once she said, 'I pulled the manual apart! I'd just go through the manual, study it and then I'd apply it in the field.'

> That, to me, is the epitome of a winner: They train, they study and they have the courage to test their knowledge in the field. They know they might fail when they try new techniques. When Sandy tried and failed, she studied the manual again, went back out and tried again ... until she got it right.
>
> Fast forward 15 years, and she has built a great life for herself. She has done so as a single mum, raising her son on her own, and now she's financially secure.

Sandy Rogers is a winner—in her career and in her life.

I wonder how many real estate salespeople actually appreciate the golden opportunity their careers offer them. When you landed this career, you won the lottery. Do you need reminding how good you have it?

- *Selling dreams*: So many people dream of owning property. It is a talking point at many parties and in the media. I would go as far to say that real estate is more talked about now than the weather.

- *Freedom*: Your time is your own. Although you may have to attend sales and training meetings, you don't have a boss looking over your shoulder. Get results and most of the time you are left alone.

- *Nice clothes*: You don't have to put on high-vis vests and work in hot, dirty environments. You wear nice clothes, work most of the time in air conditioning, and if you know what you are doing, you make more money than any miner.

- *Nice car*: I'm not advocating that a salesperson leases a flashy car that ends up costing three times the list price by the time it is paid out. I prefer salespeople to buy good cars with cash. But you *can* still buy a nice car and enjoy it.

- *Satisfaction*: Salespeople can experience career highs every day when they sell a property and see the faces of happy sellers and buyers. For both sellers and buyers, the process of selling, buying and moving home can be traumatic. What a great feeling it is to help people and get paid well for it!

- *Huge income potential*: I've put this last because most people put income low in their lists of the most important things they want from a career. This doesn't mean money isn't important; it is just that many people have other priorities. Let's face it: Money is a reward for service. The better trained you are and the more people you serve *competently*, the more money you make.

With such great opportunities, you would expect that more people would succeed in this career, but sadly many do not. Opportunity is not always obvious — you have to look for it.

While the benefits I have just highlighted apply to real estate, the same principle applies to any career: *look for reasons to appreciate the work you do.*

If you love what you do, you will learn how to do it better — to excel at your work. Your income will increase as your competence increases and in proportion to the value you give your company. Most jobs offer opportunities for valuable people to advance.

But opportunity alone does not make you a winner. It gives you the *potential*, but it is just the starting point.

This book will help you grasp that opportunity, avoid the pitfalls and learn the proven path to success.

My background

Hundreds of books have been written about winning and success. Why should you trust me?

Every book is a distillation of the author's experiences, inspirations and learnings. This book contains my thoughts on why winners win, based on my experience working with winners.

I have spent three decades interviewing winners in my role as a sales trainer, sales leadership trainer and sales management trainer. In this book I have brought together all I have seen people do wrong and right.

Over those 30 years I have talked to more than 10 000 people. I have been coaching winners since 1993, and have analysed the data from these salespeople to find out what has held them back. I have been recording interviews with winners since 1995, asking them about their careers, why they do what they do and how they achieve the results they do.

I have also attended thousands of hours of seminars with some of the best speakers and teachers from around the world. I have learned from their wisdom and insights, and subsequently helped thousands of people put them into practice.

Why is this book different?

There is a lot of information available out there—some of it even free—but much of it is not the *right* information.

In real estate, for example, some people continue to push print media as a viable marketing tool, even though they should know print is dying—or already dead! Upon investigation, you discover they are on the board of a newspaper.

Even if they promote online marketing, their advice can be biased. I once heard an agent announce a goal for his company to 'dominate the digital space'. He planned to do so by buying premium advertising on a major property portal, later admitting he was a board member.

A lot of information is put out by people who have neither practical experience nor training, so they recycle what they have read in books. But they have not actually applied the advice they offer in the field and have therefore not learned from experience.

I take pride in the fact that in our company, Pittard, we walk our talk. There is nothing in our manuals that is not consistent with what we do in our company. None of our people say, 'Do this, just because it is a good idea.' Our speakers and trainers (myself included) have done it themselves, and probably have made the same mistakes as the people in our audiences. We aren't theorists.

The knowledge we share we built up the hard way: by trying, failing, trying again, eliminating what does not work and repeating what does work.

I have taken the best of that knowledge to share with you in this book.

Overview

Broadly, winners win because they follow this four-step success journey:

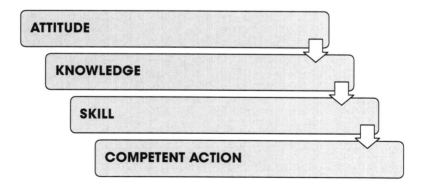

In this book, I'll teach you these four steps and show you how to use them on your own success journey. Here is a brief overview of what you'll find here:

Part I begins with a review of the common obstacles to achieving consistent results. Chapter 1 focuses on what *not* to do, because it will help you avoid the traps and mistakes that many people make. Chapter 2 looks at the qualities of winners — the things they bring to the table that make them successful.

Part II gets to the meat of the book: the success journey, and how to navigate it. Chapter 3 briefly introduces our four-step path to success. Chapters 4 to 7 explore those four steps in detail.

Finally, in Part III I share my thoughts about wealth, happiness, giving back and other matters that are the hallmarks of real winners.

I hope you enjoy the journey and I wish you all the success you deserve.

PART I
LOOK INWARD: SOURCES OF FAILURE AND SUCCESS

. . . .

WHY CONSISTENT RESULTS ARE NOT ACHIEVED

Winners come in all shapes and sizes, but most have certain characteristics and qualities that ensure their success.

Conspicuously absent are certain qualities that are common to most mediocre performers, and we'll explore these first.

If you intend to become a consistent top performer, it will help to recognise the poor habits that contribute to low or inconsistent results. Some of these are work habits; others are thought and attitude habits.

The four fatal flaws

The main factors behind poor performance are what I call the 'four fatal flaws'. If you find you identify closely with these habits, it will almost certainly indicate that Sales is not for you. They are:

- low ego drive (self-esteem)
- wrong career selection

- little belief
- call reluctance.

People who suffer from these 'afflictions' often go through the motions, but their chances of long-term success are nil.

Winners represent 20 per cent of the total sales force but account for 80 per cent of total sales volume. The other 80 per cent of the sales force fight it out for the remaining 20 per cent of the sales.

No wonder life is tough for those who find themselves in this 80 per cent. The truth is, they're in the wrong career!

Low ego drive

This is known as the *care–close* combination: Successful salespeople strike a fine balance between caring for their customers and closing the sale (the persuasion factor). Depending on the product you are selling, the balance will be tipped one way or the other, but it must never be totally devoid of care.

For example, the person managing rental properties and the person selling residential properties are both salespeople, but they are likely to have different care levels.

Property managers need a higher level of care because they're dealing with landlords and tenants more frequently and over a longer period of time. The relationships between property managers and their clients last longer than the relationships between sales agents and their clients. Property managers also have fewer closing opportunities than sales agents. Managing rental property requires a higher *care* and lower *close* balance.

Property salespeople must also display a high level of care for their clients. Although they represent property sellers, they still have an obligation to care for their buyers, to give honest advice and never to conceal information buyers should know. They must also close the sale when it is appropriate to do so. Compared with property managers, sales agents have a lower *care* and higher *close* balance.

The desire to succeed can be seen clearly in the following example of two contrasting salespeople.

The first salesperson, Adam Horth, did not come from a wealthy home. After moving from Sydney to Brisbane in search of opportunity he started working in a real estate agency as a prospector and was determined to do the best job he could.

In two years Adam averaged 15 listings a month. He worked at getting better: He studied at night and practised what he learned in the field. In the first year his leads generated $450 000 in fees; in the second year, $720 000. Adam studied, practised, worked hard and improved.

The second salesperson—let's call him Stephen—joined the agency around the same time as Adam. This young man had also moved from Sydney in search of opportunity. Adam invited Stephen and his partner to join him and his partner for dinner. They were due to meet at 7 pm, but only Stephen, his partner and Jess, Adam's partner, showed up at the restaurant. Jess assured them Adam would be there as soon as he could, and sure enough he arrived at around 7.30—with a listing.

Two salespeople: One went home, changed, picked up his partner and arrived at the restaurant on time, but with no result. The other focused on getting a result *and* going out for dinner, still in his suit and only a little late.

I'm not saying you must put work ahead of family and friends, but Adam was driven (he has a high ego drive) and results were important to him. He had to close the sale to meet his personal target.

Being a successful salesperson requires a passion for persuading people to buy from you, and it was a passion that Stephen didn't have at that stage of his life. I didn't either when I started. But I worked hard, trained, practised and steadily improved. I developed this strategy after I attended a Tom Hopkins seminar and bought his book. I studied all 62 of his closing strategies until I knew them by heart. I implemented them and refined them, learning from both my successes and my mistakes.

Wrong career selection

Do you think you are in the wrong job?

When I started in Sales, I didn't think I would like it. But when I looked back over all the jobs I had had, I realised they were just jobs, not careers. Every time I was unhappy with what I was doing, I left and found something else that interested me.

Sales only became my passion after I knew what I wanted to do with my life. Then I worked at it and came to love it. Along the way, I learned not to give up on something just because I wasn't good at it, but to learn all I could and *then* decide whether or not it was right for me.

If you are looking for a job with a regular income, Sales is not for you. It is hard on people who don't have the ego drive necessary to make it a successful career. Sales is not for the faint-hearted. Facing rejection after rejection is not easy, but if you learn to handle it, to study, practise, improve and work hard, you may just forge a successful career. So before you decide that it isn't for you, first try getting good at it. You need resilience.

Sales is not for job seekers. If you are looking for a job, do something else. If you are in Sales now and treating it like a job, I suggest either changing your attitude or changing jobs.

Sales is a career, not a job. Believe me, there is a huge difference between a job and a career.

Here are the *Macquarie Dictionary* definitions:

job: 1. *A piece of work; an individual piece of work done in the routine of one's occupation or trade.* 2. *A piece of work of defined character undertaken for a fixed price.* 3. *A post of employment.*

People with jobs work for people. They're paid an hourly rate. They work for other people's goals.

career: 1. *A general course of action or progress of a person through life, as in some profession, in some moral or intellectual action.* 2. *An occupation, profession, etc. followed as one's lifework.*

Look at these phrases: 'progress of a person through life'; 'followed as one's lifework'. These are poles apart from a 'job'.

When I see salespeople 'working' only 9 am to 5 pm, and then complaining about how tough things are, I think, 'You are wasting a golden opportunity. Stop acting like a paid worker and start acting like a self-employed entrepreneur. Get out and look for business!'

Little belief

I agree with Brian Tracy when he says top professional salespeople believe themselves capable of being the very best in their fields. This belief comes from knowledge and understanding, which come through studying and practising — *learning* how to sell.

You have to believe in what you are selling. If you don't, you will never present with conviction and passion, and your ability to persuade will be greatly diminished. You cannot believe in something you don't understand, and you won't understand something unless you study it. See the pattern?

There is nothing your competitor can do that you cannot do better through training. For example, in the real estate industry, many salespeople lie to get the listing. Dealing with lying competitors is a challenge we have to overcome, and you can only do that effectively with training. The antidote to lying is to focus on what the seller wants, which is to know the truth about what the market holds for them. (That is, don't tell them just what you think they want to hear.)

When you totally believe what you are telling them, and you deliver the truth tactfully, you will be successful in getting their business. Truth is a great sales tool, and you never have to lie or compromise your values just to get the business.

Call reluctance

In *The Little Red Book of Selling*, Jeffrey Gitomer suggests that by far the biggest fear for salespeople is fear of failure. It has a cousin: fear of rejection. Rejection is the pathway to failure — if you fear it.

Fear needs to be faced. You cannot overcome fear by simply reading about it. You cannot overcome your fear of spiders by reading how to handle spiders; you have to handle a spider to move past your fear.

Self-help books telling you how fantastic you are will not help if you are scared of prospecting. You have to go out and 'do' the prospecting, and that will banish your fear of it.

Some salespeople spend too much time preparing to work and not enough time working. Too much preparation is fear in disguise. You might give it another name, such as laziness or procrastination, but it is still fear. While you are 'preparing', you are not doing what you fear — prospecting.

Other reasons

The Four Fatal Flaws are certainly deal-breakers, but they aren't the only obstacles to getting consistent results. Knowing yourself well enough to recognise those other flaws will enable you to work on them and overcome their impact on your success.

No goals

Most people spend more time planning their holidays than they spend planning their lives. They don't set goals, and they certainly don't set SMART goals, as taught by my friend Dr Denis Waitley:

- Their goals aren't *specific*, so they don't know what success looks like.

- Their goals aren't *measurable*, so there are plenty of grey areas.

- Their goals aren't *achievable*, so it is easy to lose focus and motivation.

- Their goals aren't *realistic*, so it is too easy to find excuses for giving up.

- Their goals aren't *time-bound*, so they either don't have sufficient time or have too much time, making it easy to procrastinate.

No plan

Mack Hanan says, 'If you don't have a plan, stay in the car'. It's said half the salespeople who enter Sales fail. The general reason given is they have a lousy attitude. But are the other 50 per cent great salespeople? Some are, but most have low ambition and fall into the mediocre category. They keep their jobs because they have a pulse and do just enough to avoid being fired. *They are mediocre by choice.* Mediocrity is a (subconscious) choice that comes from inaction or too many wrong actions.

Salespeople who don't reach their targets have also failed. Did they fail because they had a plan that didn't work? Did they fail because they had a plan but didn't follow it? Or did they fail because they didn't have a plan in the first place? One hundred per cent of the time, they failed because they didn't have a proper plan.

Among this group there are also great salespeople. This elite 20 per cent write 80 per cent of the business. They are great by choice. Greatness is also a choice that comes through large quantities of the right actions performed consistently and competently over time.

Successful salespeople follow a solid plan. They carefully think about what they want to achieve and how to achieve it. They plan where their business will come from, know how many people they're going to speak to and the quantity and type of marketing they will distribute. Salespeople who follow this type of plan are almost certain to succeed.

Poor time management

Time management is a myth. You cannot manage time. You have the same amount of time as anyone else, and you cannot manage it to get more minutes. The only thing you can do is manage *yourself* within the time you have available.

People who manage their time poorly pretend to be busy, wasting valuable time in the process, but it often doesn't take much to fix their poor habits. For example:

- If you are chronically late, leave earlier.
- If you think it might take an hour, allow an hour and a half.
- If you are going to an appointment, allow double the time it will take you to get there. If you arrive early, door knock until it's time for you to go in and get that listing.

If you have been a poor time manager for some time, why haven't you learned to manage your time properly? I started studying time management in 1990 and I haven't stopped. Decades later I'm still finding ways to do things differently and to work smarter.

Winners achieve big goals because they take many small, but effective, actions. A trick I learned from David Allen, in his book *Getting Things Done*, is to break down every project into individual actions. He advises us to work only on the next action for each project. Complete that action and then move on to the next. This one tactic has helped me to complete many complex projects without ever feeling overwhelmed. You don't have to worry about an entire project, other than determining a deadline for its completion and breaking it down into smaller tasks.

If you execute your actions by effectively managing yourself within the time you have available, you will achieve success. If you keep failing because you haven't taken action to manage your time properly, all you are doing is feeding your low self-esteem. Low self-esteem prevents you from learning how to become successful and from performing the actions necessary to succeed. Subconsciously, people with low self-esteem believe they don't deserve success.

Minimum effort

Minimum effort means you are doing just enough to get by. Sales is stressful for people who invest minimum effort because they don't want to work. How demotivating is it to go to work thinking you might get fired for not doing the actions expected of your role?

I don't believe in firing salespeople for not generating money, but I certainly believe in firing salespeople for *not doing the actions that generate money*. I know that if there is no action, there is no hope; without action, there can be no results. I want results. I pay salespeople to take the right action; and if there is no action, that person must leave.

You might think this harsh, but is a boss wrong for insisting on the actions and results she's paying for? And is it fair to take money from a company and not carry out the actions you are paid to do? Inaction is a conscious choice. Mediocrity is self-inflicted.

11

Not getting it

Too many people think Sales is a job. It isn't. Sales is a profession and it needs to be treated as one.

For example: Salespeople present a listing but they don't understand marketing. Because they don't understand it, they cannot present it with enough passion to make the sellers confident they are getting a 21st-century, cutting-edge marketer. What they get instead is a hack who parrots things they heard at a seminar but never really understood.

You might have heard the saying, 'I hear, I forget. I see, I remember. I do, I understand.' When I started out I studied hard. I often got it wrong but I learned to be better. Too many people don't want to put the hard work into getting it right.

In *6 Habits of Highly Effective Bosses*, Stephen Kohn and Vincent O'Connell quote Dr Eric Maisel: 'Your listening skills, life experiences and intuitions about human nature come together and help you read people.'

Is there any more valuable skill than this in Sales? Some people study and learn this skill, but others cannot be taught. These people just don't care enough to do what it takes to be great. Empathy comes from study, thought, understanding and love of the industry in which you work. All of these develop over time.

Erratic focus

In *Million Dollar Habits*, Brian Tracy argues that the more you discipline yourself to concentrate single-mindedly on your most important task and stay with it until it is done, the more energy you'll have.

There is a saying: 'If you want to get something done, ask a busy person.' Busy people are good at getting things done because they are organised, work on the right activities and are efficient.

Despite being told a job would give me security, the more I learned about selling, the more I realised my security came from my marketability in the workplace, not from a job somebody gave me. By focusing on Sales and getting good at it, I carved out a wonderful living for myself and my family.

Not conscientious

Many salespeople aren't conscientious enough to learn and grow within their role. They take money under false pretences: They are the first to complain if their salaries are banked a day late, but can they honestly say they have earned their salary when they don't produce the results to justify what they are paid?

When you board a bus, you buy a ticket and you expect the driver to drive you to your destination. You don't expect him to sit there and say he knows what he's supposed to do, but he just isn't doing it. It's the same with salespeople. If you know what you are supposed to do, you'd better do it—otherwise that space will be filled by someone who is going to deliver and justify their pay.

Commercial space is sold or leased by floor area. Salespeople occupy about five square metres of commercial space, so if you are going to occupy that space, you have an obligation to make it return an income for your company. If you aren't comfortable with that, find something else to do, because that is part of the job description.

If you're not conscientious and are taking a salary under false pretences, I call that theft.

Summary

As you can see, there are many reasons why people don't achieve consistent results on their path to success.

If you recognise some of these faults in yourself, don't give up! It doesn't mean you *cannot* succeed; it just means you haven't been doing what you need to do in order to be successful. You now know what is holding you back. Work on your weaknesses. If you keep tolerating them, they will keep you from greatness.

Be especially careful if you recognise one of the Four Fatal Flaws in yourself. In my experience, people with these characteristics struggle in their work. It doesn't mean they will never succeed, but they have a lot of work to do to overcome these flaws.

What's next?

We have examined what causes people to fail, but what makes them succeed? In the next chapter, we will look at this side of the coin: the qualities that make winners win.

WINNING QUALITIES

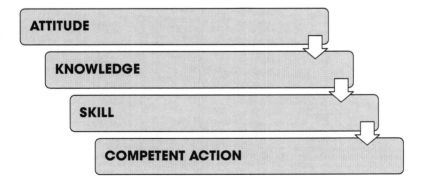

The main reason winners win is that they *want* to win. They define what success means to them and they go after it. They have the desire to win. They study, they develop knowledge, they practise and they learn the skills required to achieve excellence. They're willing to do whatever it takes to develop the qualities necessary to win.

Winners look inward, critically examine their abilities and work to eliminate unproductive habits and qualities and replace them with productive habits.

In this chapter, we'll look at winning qualities in each of the four stages of the success journey:

ATTITUDE

KNOWLEDGE

SKILL

COMPETENT ACTION

Attitude

Never underestimate the power of attitude. The right attitude opens you to life's possibilities; the wrong attitude leads to excuse-making.

Self-discipline

In *Million Dollar Habits*, Brian Tracy notes a direct relationship between self-discipline and self-esteem. The more you discipline yourself to behave in a certain manner, the more you will like and respect yourself.

This starts with setting goals.

> Some time ago, when I was on my way to going broke and owing $511 000, I set goals and put my plan in place. I immediately felt better about myself and my situation, because I was in control. I could control the amount of money I earned and what I could put towards paying off that debt. Part of my plan was to put money aside for recreation, and I saved a portion as well. Paying off the debt would slowly decrease the burden, my recreation money gave me quality leisure time with my family, and my savings prepared us for the future.
>
> Control gave me back my self-esteem and I felt less stupid for making the mistakes I had made. I stopped beating myself up. I had a plan of action and I was putting it in motion.

Brian Tracy suggests self-esteem comes from a feeling of confidence, a quality that will allow a winner to say no at the appropriate time. He believes that without a healthy level of self-esteem, it is impossible to fully develop time management skills. You can't confidently present yourself to people without a healthy level of self-esteem, either. When the inner being is right, the outer being shines.

Reliable and trustworthy

To become reliable and trustworthy, we have to say what we mean and mean what we say. We strive to become dependable people who live up to our promises. Our word is our bond, and our sense of honour gives us a feeling of pride in our career.

Salespeople should realise that when they set a target they're also giving their word. Don't agree to targets just to shut your boss up. Do everything you can to reach those targets. In his book *There's No Such Thing as 'Business' Ethics*, John Maxwell says we make commitments with care and then have to live up to them. I have never met a leader who has built a successful team with even one unreliable person. Keeping a promise is the cornerstone of all relationships and it is absolutely essential for success in business.

Every time I make a promise I enter it in my diary immediately. I once promised someone I would do something but didn't put it in my diary, only remembering it a few days later. I did what I promised, but not when I promised to do it. I have never made that mistake again. When you make a promise, enter it in your diary and deliver when you said you would. That is how you become reliable and trustworthy.

Courage

In *Crunch Point*, Brian Tracy identifies two aspects of courage: the courage to launch and the courage to endure. I have seen plenty of people with the courage to launch, but not so many with the courage to keep going.

It takes real courage to break from traditional ways of thinking and to live up to commitments. If you come from a family that didn't have much money, it's difficult to change to setting goals and thinking about wise investments to accumulate wealth over time. People in your own family may denigrate your efforts and accuse you of being greedy.

When we went broke, some people said we got what we deserved; they said we were greedy. By that criterion, everyone in business is greedy. This is nonsense. The real reason we went broke is because we went into a business we didn't know anything about, which was stupid. But at least we had the courage to quit our jobs and have a go.

We still have a go, every day. Today we are enjoying the benefits of a bit of good old-fashioned hard work and planning. It takes courage to make the effort to be successful, every day. It takes dedication as well.

Loyalty

Be loyal to everyone who deserves it. In business, be loyal to your company, your leader and your clients. In your personal life, be loyal to your friends, partner and kids. If you give loyalty, it will come back to you.

Loyalty means you take a stand if someone badmouths a friend, colleague or family member in your presence. To me, 'office politics' is talking about people behind their backs. If someone complains to me, 'I'm having a problem with so-and-so,' the first thing we do is have a meeting with that person so they can hear what is being said about them. That is a demonstration of loyalty.

Loyalty isn't given for money or reward. Over the years, I've seen people being 'loyal' to the person paying them, but as soon as the payment ends, the 'loyalty' ends. That is not loyalty.

Loyalty isn't being blind to faults, either. My wife and I have been together for more than 40 years. She's easygoing, but if I'm doing something wrong, she will tell me. You shouldn't sit by while someone is doing the wrong thing, damaging their reputation or compromising their values.

Personal accountability

In *How to Ruin Your Financial Life*, Ben Stein advises: 'Know that there are no free lunches anywhere once your parents die. You are the primary person responsible for you, and caring for your family is a moral duty, which includes being careful with your money.'

Personal accountability means being responsible for ourselves and accepting responsibility for the fact that our decisions and actions have created our present situation. Outside forces play their part, but we are responsible for how we respond to them. Accepting responsibility means we look for solutions, not problems.

We live in a society that shirks responsibility. People complain about living in a nanny state, but in times of economic difficulty they want to be bailed out. Decide what you want and take responsibility for your decisions and actions.

We are where we are in life because of decisions we have made in the past. We can make a better life tomorrow by making better choices today.

When I think of someone like Helen Keller, I have to try hard to think of any reason why a person cannot overcome adversity and become whatever he or she wants to become.

Blind, deaf and mute after an illness in infancy, Helen Keller had no way of communicating with the outside world. She had a fine brain, but no way of articulating her thoughts. All that changed on 3 March 1887 when Helen met a teacher, Anne Sullivan Macy. With patience, love and strict discipline, Anne worked with Helen, teaching her to communicate and enabling her to unlock the huge potential stored within. Helen Keller later called 3 March her 'soul's birthday'.

When you read the story of Helen Keller and the relationship with her teacher, you cannot help but be moved by the struggle both teacher and pupil endured.

Helen went on to become a role model not only for the vision impaired but for countless others, as a journalist, educator and political activist. Her setbacks began soon after birth and continued all of her life. Helen is famous today, not for those setbacks, but for her triumph over adversity.

I accept that my decisions, good and bad, have led me to where I am today, that I played a big part in determining my present circumstances. When we accept responsibility for the fact we largely make our own circumstances, and resolve to improve our present situation, life ceases to be a struggle and instead becomes a journey of discovery.

I hear people describe life as hard and as a battle. I don't like this picture. Life gets tough at times, but it is our attitude toward life's setbacks that determines whether life is tough. I believe that even life's 'toughness' is a matter of personal choice. Winners' lives aren't without problems. It is how they handle their problems that sets the winner apart.

Problems (you can call them challenges, setbacks or failures, if you like) aren't the end of the line; they are stepping-stones to success. Some people say true success is impossible without many failures along the way. Whether you agree or not, one thing is certain: Most successes aren't the result of one fabulous correct decision, but rather are an evolutionary process of trial, error and correction.

Do you become immobilised by your problems, or do you view them as necessary stepping-stones on your path to success?

The price of success is to be paid in advance. Earl Nightingale wrote, 'You cannot say to the fire, "First give me heat then I'll give you fuel".' If you want to succeed, you must be prepared to learn, practise, fail, get up and have another go. You must be prepared to keep going — resilience is essential.

And yes, it often comes at a price, but it isn't as high as the price of quitting. Mediocrity demands no upfront payment; it can be paid 'on the drip', but it is the highest price of all. It is the price of regret: 'if only'. The thought of looking back at the end of my life and saying, 'If only ...' chills me to the bone. By then it is all too late.

We are what we have made ourselves to be. It is our responsibility. Yes, life can be tough, but a life well lived is a joy. It is all a matter of personal accountability.

Balance

Love your career, but don't allow it to consume you. Take control and rest regularly, particularly when you deserve it. Work hard, laugh a lot, and spend time enjoying your life and sharing your success with those you love. Balance your life between the professional and personal.

Some imbalance shouldn't worry you too much, but be attentive to it so you can manage it. The pendulum is never going to rest exactly vertically; it will always be out of balance one way or the other.

Sometimes you have to balance your desire for balance. During a booming real estate market, a winner said to me, 'If some idiot talks to me about balance one more time, I'm going to punch him in the head. The market is *booming!* Why wouldn't you make the most of it? This is the time to work!'

I agree with him. There are times when you have to put your head down and work, even if things get out of balance. Pay back later, but when opportunity knocks, *open the door!*

In *Success Built to Last*, authors Jerry Porras, Stewart Emery and Mark Thompson write: 'Carve out a little time each week on the job or after work to experiment in some way with one of your other passions. Spend time doing some things you really like doing—a hobby.'

John Maxwell quotes Pat Reilly in his book *There's No Such Thing as 'Business' Ethics*: 'Sustain a family for a long period of time and you can sustain success for a long period of time. First things first: If your life is in order you can do whatever you want.'

If you are spending too much time with the family and not enough time working, or the other way around, one of them will suffer.

Gratitude

John Kralik is the author of *A Simple Act of Gratitude* and a Superior Court Judge in California. There was a time when his life was an absolute mess. However, instead of looking at how bad it was, he decided to change it. He found a reason to thank someone every day, and he resolved to send 365 thank-you notes, one per day, for the following year.

He gradually saw his life improve because he focused on gratitude. He started focusing on what was important in his life, and he looked for things to be grateful for. When he expressed gratitude, people started to respond to him in a positive way.

When he changed, his situation changed. His legal practice started to turn around and began to make money. He was able to buy an apartment and in time he was offered a position as a Superior Court Judge, a position he still holds. It all began with gratitude: focusing on the good instead of complaining about the bad.

Look at all the things you have to be grateful for, and cultivate an attitude of gratitude:

- When you wake up in the morning, notice your lungs are filled with air, which means you are alive.

- You live in a nice home.

- You drive a nice car.

- Look at your partner and think how much better your life is because they're in it.

In his book *One Life to Live* Jack Collis writes, 'We will share our abundance with others because we know what we give away comes back in greater measure.'

That is gratitude.

Knowledge

Lack of knowledge is ignorance. Ignorance won't pay the bills, and it certainly won't lead to the life of your dreams. You need knowledge to achieve that.

Written goals

Jeffrey Gitomer believes you have a responsibility to yourself to achieve. You achieve a level of success you set for yourself, not a quota someone else sets for you. Note those words: 'you set for yourself'. *You* decide. No-one else will do it for you.

Set short-term and long-term goals and write them in CAPITALS in your diary or journal. The mere act of writing down a goal takes us almost halfway to its achievement!

When you set goals, think about the whole picture. What is the point of being rich if your family hates you? In *Success Built to Last*, Jerry Porras, Stewart Emery and Mark Thompson talk of the inadequacy of some dictionary definitions of success:

- 'achievement of something planned or attempted'
- 'impressive achievement, especially the attainment of fame, wealth or power'
- 'something that turns out as planned or intended'
- 'somebody who has a record of achievement, especially in gaining wealth, fame or power'.

Nowhere in these definitions, they point out, do you find any reference to meaning, fulfilment, happiness or lasting relationships. There is no mention of feeling fully alive while engaged and connected with a calling that matters to you. There are no thoughts of creating a legacy of service to the world. Yet these are the things people with lasting success say they value most in their life and in their work.

Mark Murphy argues in *Hundred Percenters* that if you look behind every truly great accomplishment, you will find a challenging goal, a goal that tried and tested people's beliefs about what was possible.

SMART goals, he says, can still be pretty dumb. Sometimes they act as impediments rather than enablers of bold action, and actually encourage mediocre and poor performance. Sometimes SMART goals don't push you beyond your resources; they don't encourage you to bite off more than you can chew; they make you play it safe and stay within your limitations. Be less focused on making sure your SMART goals are written correctly on your goal-setting forms, and ask instead if these are the *right* goals for you.

Planning

You are capable of almost any level of success, provided you devote the time to proper planning and preparation, and then follow through on the plan.

Be clear about each goal:

- Why do you want to achieve it?
- What do you have to do in order to achieve it?
- How many people will you need to speak to?
- Where will your business come from?

Then put a plan in place and follow it.

Good leaders won't allow their salespeople to fail through not having a plan. Everyone needs a plan, no matter how good they are. I have followed plans since the early 1990s, and continue to do so.

If you don't reach your targets, make a plan to change the situation. If I were your leader, you wouldn't be working with me if you didn't have a plan, because I don't want people who fail consistently. I don't want people who train themselves to be mediocre. That is what you get when you don't plan.

In *The Psychology of Sales Call Reluctance*, Shannon Goodson and George Dudley see motivation as energy: In order to work, it needs to be connected to something. What is your motivation connected to?

Ideally, you should have clearly focused career goals to support your prospecting activities, and you should be able to accomplish these goals from where you are right now. If you can't, your motivation will be disconnected from your goals. Motivation without firm supportive goals becomes a mindless struggle, and eventually your drive overpowers your direction. Prospecting becomes mechanical, tedious and boring; you are asleep at the wheel of your career. Prospecting activity will drop off, not through call reluctance but through a lack of interest.

Goodson and Dudley go on to talk about strategies. Some salespeople take pride in being able to recite their goals and ambitions. They think it impresses people. If you scratch beneath the surface, however, you won't find any substance — no thought, no purpose, no planning, just a recitation for effect. Without a plan for reaching their goals, they are easily side-tracked.

One of the first performance areas to suffer is prospecting. Salespeople who don't plan their prospecting consistently aren't call-reluctant; they're confused. They spend endless hours constructing elaborate lists, plans and strategies to achieve them, but they do little else. They devote little motivational energy to actually carrying out their plans and pursuing their targets. They would rather talk and plan than prospect and promote.

Goodson and Dudley compare being a 'driver' with being a 'striver'. During the 1970s it became fashionable to insist good salespeople had to be 'drivers'. That term hasn't aged well, because drivers didn't live up to their billing. They were valued for their motion, but no-one bothered to check their sense of direction. They were doing a lot, but they weren't doing anything that led to a result. To be successful, you need a plan.

Focusing on results

Winners are superbly focused. When it comes to minor tasks, winners adopt a program of 'planned neglect'. They develop real 'target fixation' and regularly ask if what they're doing leads directly to a result. They sacrifice doing what is good for doing what is right. They work on getting results.

Anyone can focus for a day; they can even focus for a week; but show me someone capable of focusing for a decade and I will show you a winner.

Why do people who follow the lifestyles of the rich and famous on TV live their lives vicariously through people like that? They want what they have, but they don't realise those people put in the work to be rich and famous. I don't have the skills of Michael Bublé, but I do have other strengths.

My friend Dave Hamilton owns a successful company that supplies control valves to the mining industry. We attended an inspiring talk given by the respected Australian brain surgeon Charlie Teo. Midway through the talk, Dave whispered to me, 'He's good with brains, but I'll bet he knows bugger all about valves!'

Funny, and right, I thought. Whether you are a brain surgeon, a valve expert or a great salesperson, it is up to all of us to look for our strengths, build on them and find an application for them.

Skill

Knowledge is theory. Only through practice does it become skill.

The client is number one

Design everything you do, or plan to do, for the benefit of the people for whom you act. Winners focus on what is best for their clients. This is the only certain path to long-term success and prosperity for their clients and themselves.

When selling to clients, ask questions in order to clearly understand their needs. Then only sell solutions that matter to them. To do otherwise makes us no better than con artists who make sales at any cost. Professional salespeople care enough to ask the right questions, and make recommendations designed to improve their clients' lives. If you do the right thing by your clients by giving them proper solutions, and you close them on those solutions, you will know you are in a profession that makes a positive difference in people's lives.

Jeffrey Gitomer, in his *Little Black Book of Connections*, quotes Dale Carnegie:

> *You can close more business in two months by becoming interested in other people than you can in two years by trying to get people interested in you ... Look at the customers you wish you had. The main reason you cannot get them is that somebody else has a better relationship than you do.*

Long-term success comes through the great relationships we have with the clients we serve.

Caring for people

A deep and genuine caring for people is essential in all customer service industries. Caring comes from within and cannot be feigned for long. Only those who really care about others can ever enjoy true success.

In *Little Black Book of Connections*, Jeffrey Gitomer explains that you strengthen relationships by giving value, not facts about yourself. Yet how often do salespeople begin their listing presentations by talking about themselves? Too often. In Gitomer's book *The Patterson Principles of Selling*, John Patterson is quoted as saying, 'A satisfied user is the best advertisement you could have.'

Authors Bob Burg and John David Mann, in their book *The Go-Giver*, caution us to be ever mindful of our relationships with clients, and to put their needs ahead of our desire to make a sale. 'Your true worth is determined by how much more you give in value than you take in payment.' This book is a must-read for everyone in the customer service arena.

You will be rewarded for good service and great value. Care for people; don't care about what people think of you. Caring for people doesn't mean people-pleasing. Don't just tell them what you think they want to hear while avoiding what they don't want to hear. Instead, care enough about them to tell them what they *need* to hear.

As a leader, care enough about your people to tell them if they're doing something that could lead to mediocrity. Winners are thick-skinned but sensitive to others' feelings.

Presentation

Winners look like winners. Dress better than your clients. Professional business attire is essential. Pay special attention to personal hygiene, and ensure you don't have bad breath or body odour. Use aftershave or perfume in moderate amounts. If you're a smoker, be extra careful not to smell of cigarette smoke.

Brian Tracy advises in *Million Dollar Habits*, 'You should develop the habit of cleanliness and excellent hygiene in every part of your life. Resolve to look excellent in every aspect. High levels of cleanliness and orderliness in your personal and business life will also improve your self-image and improve your self-respect. When you look good, you feel good.'

When I was going through tough financial times, I had four good-quality shirts and got two suits tailor-made. I also spent $400 on a pair of shoes. It all cost a lot of money, but every time I dressed in those clothes I felt good about myself. When I felt good, I sold better — and the investment paid off.

When you buy clothes don't buy something trendy, because it will date quickly. Buy something classic and it will last you for many years.

Have respect for yourself and your clients will show you the same level of respect.

Passionate product belief

Everyone in real estate dreams of owning their own piece of their country. You sell dreams. You have a career worth getting passionate about, so *be* passionate about it.

Winners talk real estate all the time, not just when they're selling. They create need. When you meet strangers at a party, engage them in a conversation about property, but don't just talk about yourself. Care about them and their profession so you build a relationship.

Whether it is property or another product or service you offer —or perhaps you work in a quite different organisation— what can you find to be passionate about?

Be passionate about your profession because it will come through in all your conversations.

Substance

Some real estate agents really look the part: glossy brochures, impressive marketing materials, luxurious offices, flashy cars—you know the type. Looking professional is a must, but professionalism goes far beyond appearance.

Agents who look good but who can't back it up with competent service and proven results aren't anything more than show ponies. And there are plenty out there. These people are good-looking order takers.

You can't hide behind your marketing and your company image forever. At some point, you have to impress clients with what you can really do. During your presentation, give clients compelling reasons to choose you. This must be more than just the advertising you do, because advertising is the listing tool of the order taker. You must demonstrate substance and offer real value.

> A friend told me about an agent who had been following her for 12 years. Over that time, he posted her some very expensive marketing, and to his credit he kept in touch with her by telephone too. Finally, he set an appointment for a listing presentation.
>
> And then he blew it: He was two hours late for the meeting!
>
> A basic courtesy of punctuality cost him a $20 000 fee. You could argue his hourly rate is $10 000 an hour, because that is how much he lost each hour he was late. Twelve years' effort blown by one thoughtless act.
>
> This salesperson turned out to be all gloss and no substance. A show pony.

Show ponies often believe their own press. They think they're so impressive they can get away with being late, taking shortcuts and being all show.

People aren't going to list with you because of your glossy marketing. They're going to list with *you*: and you had better be competent—substance over show.

Your success will come from making people feel at ease with you, and from your ability to convince sellers you can get them the highest prices with the least stress. Often it is the little things, such as being punctual, listening and asking the right questions, that carry far more weight than glossy handouts.

In many businesses and industries I have seen numerous salespeople of substance worried by show ponies. They shouldn't be. Study, train and let skill be your beacon of success.

Competent action

Competence trumps show.

Develop winning habits

Both success and failure are habits. The secret is to create habits that lead to success. Always ask yourself, 'Is this a habit that will make me a success?' If the answer is no, don't waste any more time on it.

I have identified several habits that lead to success:

- *Set goals:* If you don't set goals, your earnings will fluctuate from month to month, and your performance will suffer.

- *Keep score:* Keep score of successes and failures. Calculate the ratio of presentations made against listings resulting from those presentations. Cultivate the habit of counting your contacts so you can identify your weak areas.

- *Follow through:* Follow through on any potential sales. Keep a diary and enter the potential client for later follow-up.

- *Learn:* Never stop learning. If you can't learn from both your successes and your failures, you won't achieve the kind of success you think you deserve.

- *Fix it:* If you don't get a result, examine the problem and fix it. Study your presentations to see what won you the listing or what prevented you from winning it. Fix what didn't work; refine what did. If you're not getting listings, change the way you look for them. If you have been knocking on doors in established areas with few listings, change your area.

- *Think long term:* Create the habit of long-term thinking. Think of how you are going to build your client contacts over the next six months, the next year and beyond. Set your goals and plan how you're going to get there.

- *Develop winning habits:* Create the habit of focusing on results and developing winning habits.

A sense of urgency

'Do it now' is the mantra of champions. Winners control the urge to procrastinate. They identify what actions are crucial to results, and move those actions to the top of their to-do lists.

Anything you need to do must be in your diary, so you don't clutter your head with information that doesn't produce results. Prioritise and tackle the important actions first. This goes for both business and personal life. You must have a sense of urgency. Winners want to achieve their goals, so they take urgent action when required.

Superior time management

As Jack Collis puts it in *One Life to Live*, 'Time is a non-manageable resource. Our only choice is to use it, or lose it.' In *The Patterson Principles of Selling*, Jeffrey Gitomer observes that many people make the mistake of getting little things out of the way before they tackle the big things. Get the big things out of the way first and then the little things will disappear.

In *Million Dollar Habits*, Brian Tracy writes, 'Developing the habit of starting on your most important task and staying with it, until it is 100 percent complete, is a great time saver.' This is critically important advice.

The late Jim Rohn is quoted by Jeffrey Gitomer in *Little Black Book of Connections*: 'Simple self-disciplines repeated over time will lead to success.' In other words, identify the important tasks and do them ... consistently.

When I was sales manager of an office equipment company, George Georgiou was one of my best salespeople. George understood the value of time. Early each working day he planned his calls and he was out selling by 9 am. He worked all day, wrote up orders, came back in the afternoon, processed the orders and went home. The next day he would be back in the office bright and early. He was a hard worker, organised, focused and caring.

If you create a program to prospect from 9 am until 1 pm, then attend listing presentations or buyer inspections in the afternoon, you will be guaranteed results. Break up your day into manageable portions and work diligently to that schedule. You will soon see a pattern of success.

Hard work

Massive action provides massive results. Once you know *how* to act, all that is left is *to* act! Too many people pretend to be busy. This gives them an excuse not to do the hard tasks that lead to results and success. You should welcome the hard tasks, as they are the price for long-term success.

Hard work doesn't automatically preclude you from having fun. But work first, then have fun. We all have lazy moments from time to time, but laziness is a habit. Once you work on the right actions, you start to enjoy the results from those actions. These results fuel your enthusiasm. If you keep moving, being busy becomes a habit.

Enthusiasm

Enthusiasm comes before success and leads to success. With your mind focused firmly on the future, you will always find a lot to be enthusiastic about. If you act as if you have already succeeded, then you will be successful. Never wait until you are 'in the mood'. Take action and the mood will be created.

The real estate business provides you with the flexibility to use your time as you please. You can choose the time you start in the morning, and you can choose what you do with your day. You help sellers get the highest prices for their properties. If you cannot get enthusiastic about this, you are in the wrong business.

Firefighters have a saying: 'If we have a bad day, somebody dies.' In *The Accidental Salesperson*, Chris Lytle discusses the concept of 'No Bad Days'. Lytle suggests that by deciding to do the right actions daily you reduce the chances of ever having a bad day. 'What if you had a job that required you to have one good day after another or else somebody would die? And that somebody could be you. Do you think you might come to work a little more focused? Would you be a little bit more "into" what you are doing?'

This is *attitude*, and a stark contrast to the mindset of the typical salesperson.

For most salespeople, a typical month is a string of bad days punctuated by the odd good day in which they're happy with their results.

Your work might not literally be 'life or death', but figuratively speaking it is. Sellers entrust you with their most valuable asset: their property. The difference between a good and poor negotiation can mean financial life or death for sellers.

If you understand that, you will be more determined to provide quality service to homeowners and buyers alike. Your job is to help homeowners realise the highest prices possible for their properties. It is also to help buyers find the right property for their needs and within their budget. Your job isn't to help buyers secure a property at a low price, but whatever you negotiate should be fair for the seller, fair for the buyer and fair for your company.

If you take this life-or-death attitude toward your negotiations, you will negotiate more professionally. If you apply the 'No Bad Days' attitude to every working day, and plan each day so you work on activities that produce results, you will reach a point where you reverse the typical sales trend. Bad days punctuated by the odd good day will become good days punctuated by the odd bad day.

It is up to you to make this happen. Sure, you can blame the market for bad days, but what good does that do you?

Take responsibility for every bad day. Look at how it happened. Ask yourself, 'Is there anything I could have done to prevent this?' Then make sure you don't repeat that mistake.

Your career can be like a cork in the ocean, being tossed wherever the current goes, or you can take control. Plan each working day. Decide on the result you will achieve that day, plan that day, then competently work toward achieving that result. Chris Lytle calls this 'selling on purpose'. You achieve results because you decide to do so, and not because some mysterious presence called 'the market' allows you to.

Bad days sometimes happen because of bad luck, but they usually happen through lack of planning and lack of skilled action on the right activities. It doesn't have to be this way.

Persistence

At the heart of every unsuccessful or mediocre person is a quitter. Resolve to persist no matter how tough things get. Persevere. Keep getting up!

In *Crunch Point*, Brian Tracy says, 'Before success comes in any person's life, they are likely to meet with much temporary defeat and perhaps some failure.'

When defeat overtakes a person, the easiest and most logical thing to do is to quit. John D. Rockefeller said, 'I do not think there is any other quality so essential to success of any kind as the quality of perseverance. It overcomes almost anything, even nature.'

Persistence is one of my favourite attributes. Set goals, plan, study, apply what you learn and persist with the right actions. Do this, and success is inevitable.

My late friend Bede Donovan used to say, 'Don't quit before the miracle happens.' I heard him give this advice often to people who were discouraged. And he was so right. How often have we seen new salespeople prospect for months, generate few leads, become discouraged and quit—and then…clients begin calling. They quit before the miracle happened!

I have heard of salespeople at listing presentations being told by sellers, 'We never make decisions quickly, so we won't be signing anything today,' and this has put the salesperson off attempting to close the sale.

The correct response is, 'I promise I won't ask you to do anything that isn't right for you,' and then proceed with your presentation. At the right time, close! Put the agreement in front of the clients, explain it to them and pass them a pen. Ask them to sign the agreement.

Ninety-nine times out of a hundred, the clients will sign. Why? *Because they want to sign.* You did a good presentation, answered their questions and filled them with confidence. You earned the right to close, regardless of what they said earlier.

Even if the clients say you are leaning too hard, apologise and say, 'I'm sorry, I didn't mean to come across as pushy. It is just that I thought you were happy I could do a good job for you. Was I right?'

'Yes,' they will admit.

'And am I right in thinking you do want to sell?'

'Well, yes.'

'Would you want a salesperson working for you who was afraid to close buyers or to ask them to pay more? I think you want someone who will ask for the order, don't you?'

Again they will agree, and you will have earned their respect.

'Right, so if you can okay the agreement just there, I can get to work finding a buyer for you.' And you hand back the pen with a smile.

Ask another question. Try another close. Knock on another door. Ask for the order. Every time. Without fail.

Persistence pays. Keep going—you aren't a quitter.

A realistic mental attitude

It is very hard to maintain a positive attitude without the risk of mental damage. Handle adversities with stoicism, knowing they are merely a test of your ability to keep going. Setbacks strengthen you and are good for your soul. Know that, despite setbacks, in the end you will win.

Be realistic. It won't always go well, but your strength comes from knowing that and dealing with reality. Devise a plan and put it into action. If you haven't sold anything by the middle of the month, get some price reductions. Put some buyers in the car and do some prospecting.

Face reality and work on positive action that will yield results. Understand that things don't always go the way you want them to go, but deal with them. Don't let them get you down.

Strive to improve

No matter how effective you are, constantly search for better ways to do everything. Winners are obsessed with learning and they learn more every day. Associate with other success-bound people and take advice from those who are truly successful.

When I went broke, I spoke with a financial planner. I don't know why, because I had no finances to plan with, but he said, 'I really admire your attitude. With all of this going on in your life, you've got a good positive attitude—you are going to work and you are selling.' I replied, 'What do we train for?'

There is a saying: 'In calm waters every ship has a good captain.' Don't train for the calm waters; train for the times when it gets tough. It was tough then and I had to rely on my training to pull me through. I fell back on my training, my goals, my plans. I'm striving to improve all the time—we call it 'smart laziness'. Find a better way to do things.

Summary

Winning qualities will keep you focused and happy, with an attitude of service and an eye on long-term success. They will give you purpose and contribute to your overall happiness and sense of wellbeing. These winning qualities don't just make you a great salesperson; they make you a good person. They complete you as a human being.

What's next?

You might already recognise some of these winning qualities. That is a good start, but knowing isn't enough. It's what you do with what you know that matters.

Now it's time to look at the success journey in more detail.

PART II
THE SUCCESS JOURNEY

ANYTHING BUT 'OVERNIGHT'

Ask any successful person for their story and none will say they were an overnight success. Success is a journey. It's a journey many people have taken in the past, and you can take it as well.

There is no such thing as a natural-born anything. Some people have natural abilities, but they are only of advantage if you develop and use them. You might understand the winning qualities reviewed in the previous chapter, and know how to avoid the traps and pitfalls discussed in the chapter before it, but as with most things, knowing isn't enough. It's what you do with that knowledge that matters.

Catherine DeVrye writes in *Hope as My Compass*, 'The only place for a "what-if" analysis is in a spreadsheet. There's absolutely no point being shackled by the past. Life is never about "what-ifs", life is only about "what-is". It's about what is happening now. What is my life like today?'

The four-step path

Winners win because they follow the four-step path of the success journey:

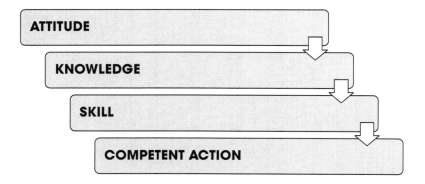

In the next four chapters, we'll look at each stage in more detail:

- *Attitude:* It all starts with the right attitude! This alone isn't enough, but it's an essential first step, because it gives you the internal motivation to keep going.

- *Knowledge:* The next step is knowing where you want to go and how to get there. This means having a blueprint (a 'big picture') for your life, creating goals along the way, setting challenging but realistic targets, and making plans to achieve those targets.

- *Skill:* The next step is to acquire the necessary skills to put those plans into action. This book is about being successful in business and in life, so although this chapter focuses on sales skills, the lessons can be applied in all types of situations.

- *Competent action:* Finally, we look at how to put your skills into practice by taking action.

The first three steps—attitude, knowledge and skill—are important, but they aren't enough. You might have the right attitude, acquire the knowledge and think you have the skill. But without action—*competent* action—you won't learn the skills you really need.

To learn to fly a plane I can read books and play Microsoft Flight Simulator, but that alone won't be enough. No amount of theoretical knowledge will prepare me for how the plane actually handles on take-off, on landing or in a crosswind. If I want to be a competent pilot, I need real-world practice. I need to get out there, fly some circuits, land—and have the instructor take over before I kill us both. However well I have mastered flying in theory, only through action can I acquire the skill needed to land a plane safely. Knowledge comes through study. Skill comes through purposeful practice.

That's why all four stages are important. Some people stop after just one or two stages, and they wonder why they don't succeed.

I've seen people stop at knowledge; we call them 'Professors'. They can quote anything out of a training manual, but they don't get results because they don't do sufficient practice to turn their knowledge into skill.

Others jump straight into action, without first building up their knowledge and practising until they develop skill. These people often think they're skilled, and many work hard, but they are hardworking incompetents.

Many people start by taking *incompetent* action before they realise they need more skills. That's all right, as long as you don't take too long to realise your actions are incompetent. As long as you're willing to learn and try again, it is a natural way to learn and grow.

The success journey is a never-ending cycle. When you do the action and it doesn't get the results you expect, you realise you need more skills. Dedicated winners return to study and practice. These people have the right attitude, are always learning and practising, and keep getting better.

Although there are only four main stages to the success journey, that doesn't mean you'll master them all at once. In *The ONE Thing*, Gary Keller and Jay Papasan explain:

> *When you see someone who has a lot of knowledge, they learned it over time. When you see someone who has many skills, they were developed over time. When you see someone who has done a lot, it was accomplished over time. When you see someone who has a lot of money, they earned it over time.*

Be patient but persistent. Time is one of your tools for learning—use it wisely.

Certain things in your life won't become apparent until you have time for reflection. For example, when I went through financial trouble, I started to work on myself and identify the things holding me back. In this way I learned to see the abundance in my life. When I became a better person, I worked better. I found more clients who were happy to pay for the service I gave them.

Getting started

Your journey to winning begins with a crucial step: *getting started.*

In *The ONE Thing*, Gary Keller and Jay Papasan quote Mark Twain: 'The secret of getting ahead is getting started. The secret to getting started is breaking your complex overwhelming tasks into small manageable tasks and then starting on the first.'

In *Crunch Point*, Brian Tracy suggests, 'The only real antidote to worry is purposeful action in the direction of your goals.' If you start working in the direction of your goals, you start to feel more in control and there is less worry.

So let's start with the first of these four stages: Attitude.

ATTITUDE

Roger (not his real name, for reasons that will soon be obvious) was a well-trained salesperson with superior technical knowledge. His presentation style was a little wooden, but he still wrote orders. However, his big weakness was that he was lazy and always tried to find an easy way to do something.

Roger did just enough to get by. He would go through the service records of the photocopier company where he worked to identify the ageing machines. Then he would talk to clients about upgrading. The trouble was, with this approach he would eventually run out of clients with machines to upgrade. What could he do then? He would have to do what everyone else does, which is to go out and prospect.

However, Roger wouldn't do that. When the well of service records dried up, he left the company. Slowly he worked his way through the service records of every photocopier company in Sydney. He even went to some of them twice. He was highly trained and knew every opposition machine, so from a technical perspective Roger was superior.

(continued)

47

What a salesperson you would have if you put all that knowledge into a hard worker! But Roger wasn't a hard worker. He hopped from job to job, eventually wearing out his welcome at all Sydney's photocopier companies. When that happened, Roger moved on to other industries. But he always looked for the easy way and never lived up to his potential.

I saw Roger waste the best years of his life, all of his training and all of his potential. There is no easy way to success, as Roger, now in his mid sixties, knows only too well. You can't eat talent.

There's nothing wrong with trying to find an easier way to do things; but if it's a choice between the easy way or no way, that is a recipe for disaster.

What's the point?

Success is an *attitude*, which is the first of the four steps in our success journey:

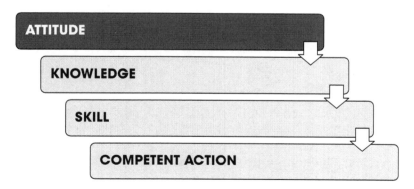

Mark Murphy talks about attitude in his excellent book *Hiring for Attitude*: 'They [great leaders] know no matter how skilled an employee may be, if a bad attitude is part of the package, that person is not a Hundred Percenter, and there are no exceptions to the rule. HARD goals aren't achieved by Hundred Percenter skill alone. They also require the Hundred Percenter attitude.'

He points to other reasons for failure:

- *Failure due to poor emotional intelligence (23 per cent):* Employees lack the ability to understand and manage their own emotions and to accurately assess others' emotions.

- *Failure due to lack of motivation (17 per cent):* Employees lack the positive attitude that fuels the drive to achieve their full potential and to excel at the job.

- *Failure due to the wrong temperament (15 per cent):* Employees have the wrong attitude and personality for a particular job and work environment.

William James said, 'It's one's attitude at the beginning of a difficult undertaking which, more than anything else, will determine its successful outcome.'

Do you want to be a great salesperson? Are you willing to do what it takes to be a great salesperson? Only you can answer these questions.

Sales isn't a game for the half-hearted, yet this is how many people approach their sales career. They have a job mentality, doing just enough to get by. They have no intention of being an acceptable salesperson, let alone a great one.

If their children had the same attitude toward their schooling, these salespeople would be the first to lecture them about the importance of learning and studying hard. They don't want their children to embrace mediocrity, but they do exactly that in their own career.

'I'm consistently amazed and disappointed,' says Jeffrey Gitomer in his *Little Red Book of Selling*, 'at the small number of people willing to execute the simple daily self-disciplines needed to reach higher levels of success. They know what will bring them the success they dream about, yet they fail to execute.'

He goes on to explain, 'Let me give you a big clue, the only way this is going to happen is with self-inspiration, self-determination and hard work that starts before everybody else gets up and continues long after everyone else has gone to sleep.'

This is self-inspiration. Not expecting someone else to do it for you, but inspiring yourself. It's about self-determination and hard work. The same people who urge their children to do well in school or their own careers don't practise what they preach.

In *Hundred Percenters*, Mark Murphy writes: 'We learned 46 percent of new hires fail within 18 months of starting the job. Unsettling to hear, but here's the part that's really critical: Out of the 46 percent of employees who fail to become any kind of acceptable performer, let alone Hundred Percenters, only 11 percent of the time a lack of technical ability, or skill, is to blame. For the other 89 percent, a lousy attitude is the clear reason behind employee failure.'

Dr Denis Waitley puts it best:

> *The Winner's Edge is all in the attitude! Not aptitude — attitude is the criterion for success. But you can't buy an attitude for a million dollars. Attitudes are not for sale.*

Winners win because they have the right attitude. In this chapter, we'll look more closely at what it takes to have a winning attitude.

Deserving

Winners believe they deserve success.

Mark Murphy observes in *Hundred Percenters*:

> *It's hard to abandon your quest for greatness once you've gotten a taste. Once you've realised limitations are more fluid*

than fixed, that the deepest fulfilment comes from climbing the highest mountains, it's hard to go back to satisficing. When you experience the fulfilment and achievement that comes from giving 100 percent, it seems like it's difficult to go back to giving anything less.

Allow yourself to accept the good things in life, and be grateful for them. Don't think, 'Why me?' Why *not* you? Why shouldn't you have the best your career can offer you?

When someone gives you a compliment, you don't have to return the compliment with something like, 'Well, thanks very much. You look really nice too.' Just smile and say thank you. Be gracious in accepting the good things in life.

Some people have a *poverty consciousness*. They cannot believe they deserve any of life's little luxuries. This is usually linked to low self-esteem. Either one on its own is enough to put the brakes on anyone's journey to greatness, but together they make it even tougher to succeed.

Such people rarely set goals or formulate plans, and even if they do, they do so half-heartedly. So when they inevitably fail to reach their 'goals' they can say, 'See, I tried that but it didn't work'.

Over the years, I have seen many people come and go in the real estate industry, but I have seldom seen any who were truly about success over the long term. Most allowed something to hold them back, and often it wasn't an unwillingness to work hard.

Never let anyone put you down and convince you that you cannot succeed. You *can* succeed, but it takes more than hard work.

Design your own vision of success. Make it a complete picture, taking in not only material wealth, but also the things that truly contribute to a full and happy life.

Now plan that future—to the decade, year, quarter, month, week and day. Set goals, write affirmations and work hard every day on the actions that take you closer to your vision.

Self-esteem

Problems and setbacks are normal and unavoidable. The only thing you can control is how you deal with them, and that makes the difference. What is the point of complaining that the market is up, down or going sideways? The market is what it is—it's the hand we've been dealt. Now what are we going to do about it?

Over the years, I've heard many salespeople blame a 'bad' market for their poor results. Yet I've never heard one credit a booming market for their success.

'Congratulations, Susan, you've written a lot of business. You must be so proud of yourself.'

'Oh, it's not me, it's the boom. Anybody can do well in this market!'

You can't have it both ways. If you blame the market for your poor results, you have to credit the market when you are doing well. That's why winners never blame the market.

Don't worry about things you can't change; focus on the things you can. You will be surprised to discover you have much more control than you think.

When you're working towards a meaningful goal, you feel in control and feel better about yourself. Now add the element of quality to your life: Do quality work, cut down on junk purchases and impulse buying, and buy fewer, better quality things. These are some of life's gifts. As you start to accept them, you start to feel good about yourself, and your self-esteem improves.

In *The Psychology of Sales Call Reluctance*, Shannon Goodson and George Dudley talk about role acceptance. Call reluctance can occur when salespeople believe they ought to be in a career other than Sales. Often they believe they have disappointed a significant person in their life, such as a parent. The result is guilt and shame, which make it impossible for them to derive satisfaction from their career. They are also unable to seize opportunities to prospect with genuine energy and zeal.

The authors believe role acceptance is learned early in life. The seeds are sown long before they enter Sales; it's part of the emotional baggage they bring with them. Once they enter a sales career, their days are filled with production quotas, sales training and other performance pressures.

They describe a study conducted with salespeople who have left the field that found that many were getting good results but left anyway. The study revealed that a large number of agents experienced a significant amount of conflict and unfinished emotional business with their parents. Many left because they felt pressure to do something 'more prestigious' or to 'make something of themselves'.

Because Sales isn't seen as a real profession, some people dismiss it as being not a 'worthwhile' career. But look at the people who do it properly, and look at the money they earn. You will see that Sales is a real profession for those who care enough to master it. I am so passionate about Sales that I believe it should be taught in schools.

There's a saying that 50 per cent of people who have university degrees work for people who don't have one. I had an engineer friend many years ago who was often out of work. Every time there was a downturn in the economy, he was laid off. I have never been out of work in my entire working life. Show me people with degrees, and I will show you salespeople who earn far more. I am not saying that people should not go to university and earn a degree if they love a particular field of study. But if you're doing it for the money, you may not love the field enough to pour yourself into it and become the best you can be. There will be no passion.

Craving opportunity

Some people crave security, but great salespeople crave opportunity. They don't mind taking a risk in order to better their careers.

You might see a person earning $200000 a year leave that job for another where they earn $150000 a year, but they recognise the long-term opportunity to make $400000 a year. They will take a risk, and even accept a lower reward in the short term, in exchange for the prospect of longer-term gain. People who crave security wouldn't do that—they just want a stable position.

When I was younger my mother said, 'When you leave school, go into the public service.' That might have been good advice for some people, but for me it was like a death sentence. I had to get out of there. Initially I felt uncertain, because I was leaving my secure workplace behind. But I got over it in the first hour out in the real world!

My mother's thinking was that the public service offered security. That was 1970. But how secure are public service positions today? I learned years ago that your security doesn't come from a job someone gives you; it comes from what you've learned, the skill you've developed and the value you provide.

My friend Andrew Trim believes that great salespeople crave opportunity over security. He's right: Someone who isn't prepared to take a risk won't be a good salesperson. If you are scared to lose the listing, or afraid to say no to a buyer because you *might* lose a sale, you will never do a good job for your client. You will accept any offer rather than negotiate the best possible price.

Be willing to take a risk. Be willing to say to your buyer, 'I can help you buy a home, but I can't help you steal one. If you are willing to pay a fair price, I'm willing to help you; but if you want to make an unfair offer, I can't help you.' You run the risk of them getting upset and leaving, but you have to be willing to take that risk.

Many people think the safe path is less risky, but that isn't always the case. If you want to be successful, to be a winner, the riskier path might be the safest in the long run.

Love of quality

Close enough isn't good enough — at least not to a winner. If you want success, choose quality.

This is an important lesson that applies equally to parents, students, business leaders, customer service people — and, of course, you in your professional role. Whatever you do, do it to the best of your ability.

Start by deciding what you want. You can't have everything, so choose wisely. There's an old saying: 'Be careful what you wish for — you just might get it.'

A love of quality isn't a love of quality *possessions*, it's a love of *quality*. In my early working life, I worked in the liquor trade, and I was taught by some very good publicans. If there was a cluster of lights with one bulb blown, I had to get up a ladder and change it. My boss said, 'Never tolerate one bulb that doesn't work, because it soon becomes two, three or four, and then — almost without you realising it — there's only one left and it looks like we're going broke.'

I have learned a lot from quality people over the years, by just watching how they work.

One was Warwick Short, with whom I worked in a wine bar in the 1970s. Even when customers were four deep at the bar, Warwick would constantly watch what was going on. He had an eye for the little things that made a difference.

For example, because most people are right-handed, Warwick set the bar up to suit the right handers. Whenever you poured a drink, you had to put the bottle back in place, label facing out and spout to the left. This saved only a few seconds each pour, but it added up to hours over a shift.

Warwick had an eye for quality and efficiency long before it became fashionable.

When I buy anything I do my best to buy quality, because good things last. I have a saying that drives my wife mad: 'You never have to take back the top of the range!'

A love of quality means you will surround yourself with the nicer things in life, and this does wonders for your self-esteem. I'm not suggesting you become materialistic. Buy fewer things, but choose quality. I bought a BMW in 2003, paid $100 000 cash for it and turned it in for $10 000 ten years later, but I never lost the pleasure of driving it.

Even if your priorities change, keep the love of quality. I don't feel the need to drive a car like that now. We sold the BMW, went to the auctions and bought a Commodore wagon for $23 000. I also like the feeling of having the money in the bank — a quality bank account over a quality car.

By buying fewer things, we could afford nicer things. Save up and buy quality items, and you appreciate them more. You're telling yourself and the universe that you're allowing yourself to have better things in life. These are the rewards for your work.

Buy only what you can afford. Don't spend big on credit cards — that's not a love of quality. Kez and I both come from poor backgrounds. After my mother died and we had settled everything up, my inheritance was $2.48! Occasionally Kez and I buy a ticket in the $50 million Lotto for fun, but I'm not the slightest bit interested in winning wealth. I'm very happy to work for what I get out of life and for the rewards I get from work.

Love of work

When you consider how much time you spend at work, it's crazy not to enjoy it. You sleep for eight hours of the day, work for around 12 hours (leave eight-hour days to those who want jobs), and have the remaining waking hours for leisure. So why not enjoy your work?

When I interviewed author Larry Winget, I asked him about the importance of love of work. He said that we don't have to love the work; if we accept money to do a job, we are morally obliged to do it well, whether or not we love it. I agree with him. This is where love of quality comes in: Whatever we do, we do the best job we can. We do quality work for the remuneration we receive. We add value.

But love of work is often about attitude. If we pour ourselves into our work, learn as much about it as we can and are determined to be the best we can be, we derive satisfaction from doing it well. The more you work on being better at what you do, the more recognition, satisfaction and even joy you will get from your work. Love of the work can follow.

There's joy in doing work well—and it's not about being paid for it. When I get my hedge-trimmer and lawn mower out, I spend time making the garden look great. When it's done, I stand back and look at it with pride. I'm not a gardener, but I do love my power tools, and I love the way the garden looks after I've worked in it.

Why do so many people complain about hard work? I've worked 55 to 65 hours a week ever since I left the public service when I was just under 20. I'm over 60, so I've worked those hours most of my life.

I have a great relationship with my wife, my kids seem to like me, I have grandchildren I absolutely adore, and I have lovely relationships with the people who mean a lot to me. I have just the right number of friends and we enjoy each other's company. I look at my blessings and know it's all possible even while working hard.

I travel a lot for work but when I'm home, I'm home. Kez and I go out and do things together. Working hard is no excuse for a poor relationship.

A colleague once told me he was having trouble at home. I asked him to describe to me everything he had done the day before. He said he went to work in the morning and after work he cooked dinner for his wife. I thought that was a nice start, but then I said to him, 'What was on TV last night?' He listed the programs he watched with his wife. So a great start to the evening was ruined by sitting mindlessly in front of the TV, instead of having a meaningful conversation with each other.

There is an important lesson here: If the person is not right, their results will never be right either. Get your work life and your personal life in order. Make a decent life. Use your work and the income it gives you as a vehicle to a quality life. If you love your work, you're never lazy. If you love it, you'll learn it. Winners look at normal and believe they can do 50 per cent better.

Summary

Having the right attitude is the first step on the journey to success. If you don't have the right attitude, you're doing just enough to get by. On the other hand, if you have an attitude that makes you want to be the best, you'll seek out other winners, read books, attend seminars and do the things that other people won't do.

Attitude is the springboard to success.

What's next?

If you have the right attitude, you'll crave the knowledge to be better—and that brings us to the next step.

5

KNOWLEDGE

George Georgiou worked with me in a company that sold office equipment, such as typewriters, ribbons and calculators. In his territory, George would serve all his customers, large or small, with equal conscientiousness. He would come into the office at around 3 pm, hand in his orders and go home; he followed this routine day in and day out. George was already a winner long before I met him.

I began working in this company as sales manager of the newly created photocopier department. I had three salespeople at first, but quickly reduced that to two because the most experienced person resisted training. I was now left with two inexperienced salespeople — one a former taxi driver and the other a former bank clerk.

I started them on a training program: Between 7 am and 9 am I taught them sales methods, how to demonstrate a copier and how to deliver sales presentations. George would be in the office at the same time, planning his day.

(continued)

One day George asked if he could join the training sessions, as he had never been trained to sell. He had learned everything he knew from books and from experience. Although he wasn't allowed to sell copiers, he knew he could apply the knowledge to selling other products in his range. Because of his experience and sales success, George also contributed to our training sessions, sharing what he knew with the other two salespeople.

George attended our training sessions for three months, at which time my duties were expanded to include managing his department. My sales force increased from two to sixteen, including George. All salespeople in this newly merged division could sell all inventory items, including photocopiers. George was the first from his old department to sell a photocopier because he knew how to demonstrate the equipment. A desire for education turned into an opportunity that George was quick to turn into income.

George was a consummate salesperson and never stopped learning. He retired a wealthy man and is happy in his golden years. That, for me, is success.

What's the point?

Winners work consistently at acquiring knowledge that will help them achieve their goals:

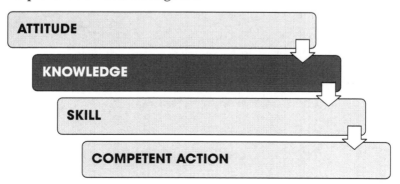

In this chapter, I will break knowledge down into specific stages (as shown in the following graphic), starting with the big picture and then drilling down into more detail.

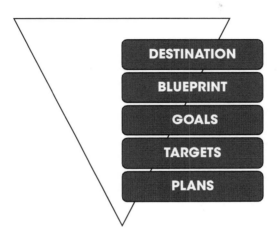

In the next chapter, we'll look at the specific skills you need on a daily basis. But those skills are useful only if you *apply* them to achieving your professional and personal goals.

Know your destination

Think about the last time you planned a journey. What is the first choice you made? The destination, of course. You would never start with the itinerary—flights, hotels, transfers or tours. The destination is your first decision.

Planning a successful career is similar to planning a holiday: The destination comes first.

Decide what success means to you. This is your destination, and it's an important decision. You don't plan a trip to Europe without first deciding which countries you're going to visit. Similarly, you can't define success without clearly deciding what success looks like to you.

Too often people believe money defines success. Don't get me wrong; money is important and I want you to have lots of it, but it's *what you do with the money* that matters more.

Would you like to be the richest person in the world but have no friends, a family who hates you and nothing but hangers-on drawn by your money? Would you call that success?

Long-term success means you have to decide what you want and then consistently work toward it. What does success mean to you? Decide. Once you have a clear, well-rounded picture of success in your mind, plan your success *itinerary*. For many, the joy is in the journey.

Decide what you have to produce in order to manifest your success picture. From these production figures, targets will emerge. Next, plan the competent action necessary to achieve those targets.

Clarity is paramount in goal setting, target decisions and planning.

If you simply start with targets and plans, you will most likely not follow those plans or achieve those targets, because you have no compelling goal — no compelling reason *why*.

You need a destination — goals — to 'pull' you toward higher achievement. Plans and targets alone won't do this.

John Wooden suggests, 'We have to make a living but we also must make a life with our family. It's easy to lose sight of that when we start chasing money and its travelling companions, fame and power.'

Plan a trip and you begin to look forward to it. Plan a successful career and you become inspired to work toward it.

Begin with a clear destination, then plan the itinerary. Enjoy your life's journey.

Blueprint your life

Too many people set only short-term goals or, even worse, have no goals at all. If you were building a house, you would have a plan. You need a blueprint for your life as well.

When I was around 36, I completed a handout from a Tom Hopkins seminar, 'My Life's Blueprint'. I did many things wrong in these early days of planning, but here is an overview of this blueprint.

In the first year I planned to earn $80 000, buy a car for $10 000 and pay $5000 off our mortgage.

By the five-year mark I planned to be earning $200 000 as an accountant (at around 40). How little I knew myself! Those who know me know I'm not a numbers person. To this day, I have no idea what I was thinking.

I also planned to spend more time with my children and take them sailing. I presume I was going to take them with me whether they liked it or not.

As I mentioned, we must be flexible and our goals must be relevant. These plans were not relevant to my children; they didn't want to go sailing. Later I adjusted my goals and we purchased a holiday property at Patonga, north of Sydney. Over a decade later we still love this property and have many treasured family memories of times spent there.

Common sense prevailed with my career choice, and I realised accounting was not for me. I eventually became a salesperson, way off the radar when I wrote my blueprint.

By the 15-year mark my goal was to consolidate our investments, and to own a 20-foot yacht and a red vintage Rolls-Royce convertible. Go figure!

I'll stop there, although the blueprint covered 25 years, by which time I would be 61 years old. But you get the idea: The blueprint was written by a 36-year-old, ego-driven male who didn't know himself very well, let alone what he and his family really wanted.

You may notice that going broke was not in the blueprint, yet that's what happened two years after I wrote it. I opened a real estate business without having a clue about how to run it. Being a photocopier salesperson and sales manager does not qualify you for success as a real estate agent.

It took a long time to haul our way out of the financial hole I had dug for myself and my family, but it wasn't until 25 years later that I came to recognise the importance of goals and blueprints.

At age 61, I looked back at the blueprint written by the 36-year-old Gary Pittard. It was more of a wish list than a set of goals, but it was the first goal setting I had ever done, and at the time I truly had no idea what I wanted for myself and my family.

I thought I was setting grand, lofty goals that would launch us toward vast wealth. But you know what? When I reviewed that blueprint recently, and compared it with where we are today, I thought, 'If we had achieved everything I put into that 25-year blueprint, I would have sold us short.' Our life today is immeasurably better—beyond my wildest dreams at age 36.

Writing a blueprint all those years ago was the beginning of my success journey. It was an important beginning, but not the plan itself.

Set yourself targets, write plans and keep on doing so until you achieve what you want. I don't mean a couple of months, or even a few years down the track—this isn't about short-term planning. I'm talking about 20 years from now. And adjust your blueprint as life changes for you.

Set clear and precise goals

I have discussed SMART goals, but according to Mark Murphy in his book *Hundred Percenters*, goals also need to be HARD—that is, Heartfelt, Animated, Required and Difficult:

- *Heartfelt:* They exist to serve something bigger than you.

- *Animated:* They must be so vivid that not reaching them will leave you wanting; there will be something missing in your life if you don't reach those goals. Most people set goals to shut their bosses up, but animated goals define your life's direction.

- *Required:* These are things that are as critical to your continued existence as breathing, water and food.

- *Difficult:* They're so hard they'll test all of your limits.

Mark Murphy identifies many reasons why people don't get excited about their goals (for example, they're not challenging, meaningful or vital to their survival). But one critical reason for goal apathy is that the goals typically sound sterile. For example, we may have a goal to make 30 sales by June 30. A goal like that is specific, measurable and time-limited but, he asks, 'Is it inspirational?'

Murphy sees HARD goals as both inspirational and aspirational. They force you to push through your self-imposed limitations to focus on something bigger than your own immediate wants, and to solve vital challenges.

The key to creating a HARD goal is to describe it so graphically that you experience it (even if just in your own mind) long before you actually achieve it.

In *Hope as My Compass*, Catherine DeVrye quotes Sir Edmund Hillary: 'What's the point of having a goal if you know you're going to make it? Where's the challenge in that?'

In real estate, if you know your own goals, you can help your sellers clarify theirs. How many times have you heard salespeople declare pathetically, 'You've got to know the seller's motivation'? You have to help them formulate their goal so clearly they can see it, even if only in their minds, long before they actually achieve it.

When they say, 'I'm not going to accept that offer—it's $20000 less than I need,' you can show them they will not achieve their goal unless they do accept it. Their choice is simple: Hold out unrealistically for more money, or accept a fair offer and achieve their goal.

If you're a leader of a team and you haven't set your own goals clearly, you cannot help your salespeople set theirs. And if you are a salesperson who has not set goals, you cannot help clients clarify theirs.

When you set a goal, attach a powerful image that motivates you toward it. This picture of where you want to be will help you adjust your plan as you go along. Set clear and precise goals, and be serious about reaching them.

Be realistic

Dare to dream, yes, but be careful—many dreams aren't realistic. I might dream I can fly like Superman, but no goal will see me achieve that fantasy. Goals must be realistic— you must have a 50 per cent chance of achieving them or you won't expend the effort needed to do so.

'If the goal is unrealistically big, and you miss it by a ridiculous amount,' writes Zig Ziglar in his classic book *See You at the Top*, 'the size of the failure would have an emotional impact for future accomplishments that could be extremely negative. It could even affect a person to the degree he would no longer really make an effort of any kind. For this reason, it is wiser to set the goal high but not out of sight.'

Setting unrealistic goals, he explains, is also an excuse to not achieve them. He talks about the 'Loser's Limp', which works like this: Athletes are competing in a race. Two of them are sprinting for the finish line, but one pulls out ahead. When the person coming second is sure he won't win, he starts to limp, feigning an injury to save face.

The Loser's Limp is just another excuse.

Next—and this is important—look at the actions needed to achieve your goals. Are they feasible? For example, a plan that called for me to speak to 200 clients a day wouldn't be feasible. I could *not* do that action. Therefore I could not reach my goals.

Goals, plans and actions must complement each other. If you do the actions competently, you reach the targets you set. Achieve the results and you receive the income. Goals should be set high enough to stretch you, and even scare you a little. But they shouldn't be set so high as to be out of sight.

Write them down

Goal setting needs to be done properly if it is to work. Statistics show only 5 per cent of people set goals, but those 5 per cent earn more than the other 95 per cent. Many people say they have goals, but they aren't written down. They are 'in their head'. This is nonsense. Goals in the head are dreams, not goals.

People who refuse to write down their goals clearly, with deadlines, aren't serious about achieving them. Because their goals aren't written down, there is no evidence they didn't achieve them. This is a perfect excuse, because no-one will know they failed.

The problem with this method is it sets you up for massive frustration. When you think you want something and then don't achieve it, frustration at not getting what you 'want' grows. It is a negative emotion that weighs you down.

It's far better to decide what you want—to calculate the income you need to earn what you want, calculate targets that will bring that income, and formulate plans to reach those targets. From the moment you do this you will have a sense of purpose, and you will feel happier.

When you set a goal you have a 50 per cent chance of achieving, you immediately feel happier.

I have never seen a person who set a goal properly fail to achieve it or at least come very close. 'Properly' is the key word.

Identify your targets

After you set your goals, identify targets to reach those goals.

Look for stepping-stones

Targets are like stepping-stones across a river. If the river is too wide for you to leap from shore to shore, you look for stepping-stones. Starting from one shore, you find a stone you can reach by extending one leg. You place one foot on that stone, test it to confirm it's stable underfoot, and reach out with your other leg for the next stone. You continue like that, stone by stone, until you reach the other shore.

Your three 'stones' on the path to success are goals, targets and plans. Setting targets without first setting goals is like trying to jump from one shore to the other without using the stepping-stones. Most people cannot stay focused on the actions required to reach high targets without clear written goals.

Leaders complain about the difficulty of getting their salespeople to focus. How many of these unfocused salespeople have clear written goals, targets to achieve those goals and a plan to achieve those targets? Had those salespeople based their targets on worthwhile goals and backed them up with firm plans, they would have found it much easier to focus.

Aim high

Adam McMahon, from Dignam Real Estate in Thirroul, NSW, writes well over $1 million in fees each year. When asked about goals and targets, Adam says, 'You have ups and downs, like everyone has. To start with, you sometimes set easy goals you think you're going to reach quite comfortably. Then over a period of time you push yourself and take your goals higher.'

Early in his career, he called another winner, Jason Hines, to ask him how to achieve big goals. Jason's advice was, 'Aim high.'

Adam told Jason, 'I can't seem to crack that hundred thousand for the quarter.' Jason's advice was to set a higher target for the quarter and plan towards achieving that target. 'You will be surprised at what happens.'

Adam did what all the winners I know do: he sought the advice of other proven winners. One phone call set Adam on the path to higher achievement.

There was a lot more to his success than one phone call, of course, but it was the first step to overcoming his perceived barrier. Before receiving this advice, Adam believed $100 000 in fee production to be a barrier. By taking his target up to $150 000, he effectively *ignored* a figure that used to be a barrier and concentrated on achieving a figure 50 per cent higher.

Setting the figure wasn't enough on its own. He also planned for it, and did the actions necessary to reach it. He made a *genuine attempt* to reach the new $150 000 production target. Your intentions must be genuine, or the goal is meaningless.

Winners like Adam McMahon earn my respect because they're serious about their careers:

- They seek advice from other winners.

- They plan their activities.
- Their targets link to clear goals and plans.
- They work hard.
- They train to improve.
- They aim high.

This is why winners like Adam McMahon are so inspiring to be around.

Make clear plans

Do you consistently reach or exceed your targets? By comparing results against targets, you will quickly identify your level of commitment. Committed, goal-oriented people set targets that stretch them—and then they achieve them.

Are you doing your best? A good way to determine this is to look at your targets and your progress toward achieving them. Your targets should stretch you and be based on reality, not fanciful thinking. Not only should you know what you will achieve in the month, but you should also plan where your results will come from. This plan will help you reach, or exceed, your targets.

In *The ONE Thing*, Gary Keller and Jay Papasan write:

> *If everyone has the same number of hours in a day, why do some people seem to get so much more done than others? How do they do more, achieve more, earn more, and have more? If time is the currency of achievement, then why are some able to cash in their allotment for more chips than others? The answer is they make getting to the heart of things the heart of their approach. They go small.*

In *The Patterson Principles of Selling*, Jeffrey Gitomer explains that if you plan your work you won't find yourself standing on the corner wondering where to go next. This is the essence of time management. Many salespeople waste time thinking about what they have to do next.

If you plan your work and follow your plan, you will end up doing the actions needed. If you work on important actions, you will bring in results.

Another gem from *The ONE Thing*:

> *We haphazardly select approaches that undermine our success. Pinballing through our day like a confused character in a B-horror movie, we end up running up the stairs instead of out the front door. The best decision gets traded for any decision, and what should be progress simply becomes a trap.*

> *When everything feels urgent and important, everything seems equal. We become active and busy, but this doesn't actually move us any closer to success. Activity is often unrelated to productivity, and busyness rarely takes care of business.*

I've already spoken about time management, and we'll discuss it again later. If you have the right actions connected to your targets, there is no possibility you will pinball through your day, and eventually your life. If you know the difference between important and urgent actions, you can plan for them properly.

Use affirmations

In *Everything Counts*, Gary Ryan Blair writes:

> *A commitment made must become a commitment honoured, as each one counts in more ways than you can possibly imagine. Your ability to honour your promises directly impacts your credibility, reputation, trustworthiness, earning ability, and overall peace of mind. Character defines an individual; honouring commitments helps to define character.*

> *If you look at successful people in any field, you may discover they're not necessarily the brightest, best looking, fastest, or strongest of the bunch. What you will find, however, is that they're the ones with the deepest reservoir of commitment. They fully understand all great accomplishment is preceded by great commitment. So, how great is the power of your commitment?*

Affirmations are commitments to your goals. Develop the habit of honouring commitments, whether to others or to yourself.

Canadian trainer Bill Nasby (BillNasby.com) taught me most of what I know about goal setting. I recommend you study his audio program *The Path to Deliberate Creation*. Bill is a great believer in affirmations.

If you're a $300 000 producer and want to double that figure, you must first think like a $600 000 producer. Written affirmations trick the mind into thinking you have already achieved $600 000.

Write your affirmation in the past tense, as though you've already achieved it. For example, I might write:

> *I, Gary Pittard, accept and enjoy that I have received $600 000 in December [year] and everything I do contributes to this result.*

Write the affirmation and sign it, 15 times a day for 21 unbroken days. You will start to think, walk, talk, act, train and present like a $600 000 producer; and when you think, walk, talk, act, train and present like a $600 000 producer, you will become one. This is why affirmations are critically important.

Study

Learn as much as you can about your profession. Become an expert. The more you learn, the more excited you become about the possibilities your career holds. You become more excited about your ability to satisfy the needs of the clients who trust you.

The more you learn, the more likely you are to feel like a true professional. You will notice, as your connection to your chosen field strengthens, that the better your results, the more passionate you become, and the more business you write.

If you don't study, you'll never learn. If you don't keep studying, you'll forget. Either way, you'll be a walking mediocrity. 'If you want to be great,' says Jeffrey Gitomer, 'learn how to get there.' If you don't want to be great, don't bother studying.

After some studying, you reach a level in training where you've heard it all before. That's no reason to stop training. The mantra of mediocrity is 'Been there, done that!' After a while, training becomes reinforcement more than learning new skills. We keep training to remind ourselves of the things we have *stopped doing* — things that used to work for us but now do not work because we have ceased doing them.

Reinforcement training is very effective because you already know the actions and how to do them, so there is no learning curve. Commence those actions and you can see an increase in your income immediately. Good training always pays for itself, even if it is mostly reinforcement.

Learn to succeed

The importance of training is underestimated in Sales. Industries worldwide are full of untrained, or undertrained, salespeople. Those who don't train are doomed to failure or mediocrity.

It need not be this way. We train so we can learn to overcome all the common barriers to sales — things like:

- rushing to make the sale, instead of putting clients' needs first

- failing to determine what is important to clients, and not demonstrating that we can give them what they need

- failing to anticipate and overcome objections, many of which are created by our competitors

- reluctance to deliver to home sellers an honest estimated price range, despite what competitors may quote

- neglecting to demonstrate points of difference to clients, thereby proving that we are the best choice

- not closing the sale.

There are more, but these and other barriers all have something in common. Winners know the answers; untrained people don't. These barriers are all *predictable*, and you can learn techniques to avoid them.

There are no new objections. Learn every likely objection and learn how to prevent it from becoming a barrier to a sale.

You might think training is expensive. It might cost $2000 to attend a seminar to learn how to overcome these barriers. But have you calculated the cost of incompetence?

Would it be reasonable to estimate that a salesperson could lose one listing per month through incompetence? If so, the salesperson loses 12 listings per year. Let's say half of those would have sold (again a conservative number). The salesperson loses six sales a year. At an average selling fee of $10 000, they have lost $60 000 in fees through lack of training. The $2000 seminar now looks like a bargain by comparison!

Although salespeople constantly hear the same objections, most are still blindsided by them. With training, they would learn how to anticipate these objections and prevent them from arising.

At some point in your sales career you should ask yourself, 'Am I in, or am I out?' Are you a professional salesperson, or are you one of the mediocre majority who don't train?

If your answer is, 'I'm in,' then you will train. Hard and often.

Be a passionate learner

In *Mastery*, Robert Greene writes, 'In order to master a field, you must love the subject and feel a profound connection to it. Your interest must transcend the field itself and border on the religious.'

It makes me wonder how many people treat their careers this seriously. I'd wager that few do. Considering that 80 per cent of business is written by 20 per cent of salespeople, I can confidently conclude only one in five people are as interested in their careers as Robert Greene suggests they should be.

Greene says you first learn your profession—this is the 'interest' part. You should be so interested in your chosen career that you learn as much about it as you can, and the more you learn, the more you realise there is more to learn. The more you learn about it, the more profound the connection you develop to your chosen field.

You become *passionate* about it. When it comes to selling any product, service or concept, passion persuades. Being passionate implies you know enough about your chosen field to become passionate about it. Passion without knowledge is fake passion.

Passion develops with time and knowledge

If you accept that being more passionate about your work would make it more enjoyable and profitable, then do as Robert Greene suggests: Love it enough to want to know more about it.

You shouldn't choose a career based on how much money you can make. Go into anything with that mindset and you will come unstuck very quickly. If you don't like it—if you're in it just for the money—you won't be bothered learning enough about it to become good at it. If you don't learn it, you won't become great. If you don't become great, you won't earn the money you thought you'd make. They don't say 'the more you learn, the more you earn' for nothing.

I didn't love Sales when I started. To be honest, some things terrified me. I found prospecting difficult, and closing. I had to learn how to do it, and then apply what I had learned in the field. I made many mistakes, but eventually I got better at it. I kept learning, and kept using what I had learned. And I kept getting better, and earning more money.

And then...gradually...the terror was replaced with the feeling, 'I could be good at this,' and finally, 'I love it!'

Be interested enough in your chosen career to learn as much as you can about it.

Love grows with time and knowledge

It's hard to love a career you're not very good at. It's also very hard to become passionate about it. Do you accept that if you loved what you do and were more passionate about it, you'd be better at it? If you do, then you must learn everything there is to know about your chosen career. Allow love and passion for your career to develop. Mastery will follow, and much quicker than you think.

Whether you are a real estate agency leader, a salesperson or a property manager, you are in the business of *Sales*. All three roles 'sell' a different product, but all require an ability to sell. So what is your primary sales concept? What is the one thing you must sell before trying to sell anything else?

You!

- If I'm going to allow you to lead me, I have to believe that by listening to you I will be better off than I am now.

- If I'm going to list my property with you, I have to believe I will get a good price with less stress than I would with any other salesperson.

- If I'm going to allow you to handle my investment property, I have to believe you are the best property manager I can get.

Selling *you* is the first sale. And the more profound your connection to your chosen field—be it leadership, sales or property management—the more likely you are to convince people to follow your advice and to do what you suggest.

Words like passion, love and profound connection border on the religious. If you were that absorbed with your career, would you be better at it? Would you be happier in your work?

Mastery is a good place to be. If you aren't there yet, learn more. Become more. Work on that profound connection.

Summary

You can break down knowledge acquisition into four parts: Goals, Targets, Plans and Affirmations. When you do these well, you will know where you want to go, and how to get there. And you will happily work at developing the skills necessary to succeed.

What's next?

Now you have your goals and plan, it's time to turn knowledge into skill to ensure you achieve your planned results. If you are not skilled, it won't matter how motivated you are by your goals, targets and plans, nor will your affirmations work. We'll consider those skills in the next chapter.

6

SKILL

I liked and admired Ross as a salesperson. He was the number three salesperson in the photocopier company where I started in Sales. At the time, I didn't know what Sales entailed. I thought the company generated the leads and all you had to do was demonstrate the machine and get the order. But Ross took me under his wing and taught me some valuable lessons.

Although he was earning $200 000 — in the early 1980s — he and his wife had only one car, which they shared during the week. When Ross didn't have the car, he would catch a ferry and work in the city showroom. When he had the car, he would call on his customers.

Ross was a terrific salesperson. He was funny and his clients liked him. He was methodical, worked hard and wasn't afraid to ask for the order. He was a fearless prospector, valued training and managed his time well. Ross was skilled.

What's the point?

When you see a capable doctor, within a few minutes you know you're in good hands. That's skill. We all know someone we can instantly recognise as skilled and competent.

Many salespeople can read a training manual and quote sections from it, but they don't have the skill to apply that material. They deliver it word for word without knowing why they are saying what they're saying—and it shows! It's like a bad actor merely reciting their lines. A good actor, on the other hand, brings a character to life.

We have now reached the third step on the success journey:

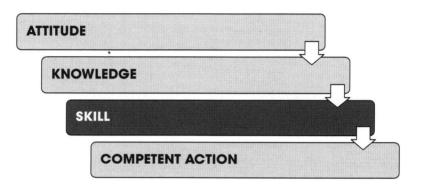

This chapter describes the most important skills you need to succeed in Sales. Some are skills you already have; others you will need to learn. Some are easy; others are more challenging. Some might come naturally to you; others take more effort.

These skills separate the amateurs from the professionals. Broadly, they fall into two areas:

- *Communicate*: Communicate properly so clients will trust you with their business. Poor communication will prevent you from being understood or trusted, closing the sale or asking for new business.

- *Convince*: Be convincing enough for the client to sign with you because they genuinely believe you know how to market their property, find buyers and negotiate a good deal for them.

There are many skills described in this chapter, and you might wonder which are essential and which are optional in Sales. Based on my decades of work with thousands of salespeople, I believe they are *all* essential.

Know your strategy

Salespeople fall into two main categories, according to their attitude and approach. Mark Murphy calls them A and B Players.

B Players are just order takers. They don't have a strategy. They reinvent the sales process for every buyer, and never learn from their mistakes or successes. For example, even when they receive the same objection repeatedly, they won't question their approach; they simply repeat it.

A Players, on the other hand, approach a sale with a proven strategy: the steps they take, the questions they ask, the things they ask for and the order in which they follow the process. Buyers change, and A Players are flexible enough to adapt, but their strategy stays the same. It works consistently because A Players know exactly what they're going to do, when and why.

Understand clients

Order takers don't persuade someone to buy. If asked, they may answer questions and describe various options, but they don't proactively create the sale. The prospect, typically induced by advertising or other means, decides on their own to make the purchase. The order taker exercises very little control.

Professional salespeople aren't order takers. They fully understand the needs and concerns of their clients, so they know the right questions to ask. By asking the right questions, they develop a deeper understanding of the problems their clients face. They then target their presentations toward showing clients that they, the salesperson, can solve those problems.

Here's a major factor in your success: Find out what people want and help them get it.

The first part (finding out what people want) is lost on order takers. They never develop a deeper understanding of their clients' needs because they jump into their presentations too soon.

Order takers confuse clients by talking as much as they can about the product or service, without first discovering what is *relevant* to their prospects. Too much information confuses people, and confused people say things like, 'I want to think it over.'

Order takers don't ask enough questions, and they don't make constructive, informed suggestions, so they miss out on sales.

I recently spent two months looking for a new office, and spoke with several salespeople. From what I saw, order takers are alive and well in the commercial real estate world, but I fear they aren't making many sales.

No-one asked me what I wanted. To this day, half of them don't know what business I am in, how and when I used my present office, what facilities I had in my present office, and what I wanted in my new office. All they had to do was ask!

Most of them showed me only the offices I asked to see. Only one suggested something different.

These agents were quoting $5000 per square metre. When I asked if they were selling anything, they replied, 'Not much.' When I suggested perhaps the price of $5000 was too high, they said, 'That's the going rate.' I said, 'But nothing is going at that rate!'

I found two buildings not ten minutes' walk from the $5000-per-square-metre buildings. I contacted two agents and made appointments to view an office in each building. I bought one that day—for just $2100 per square metre.

The first agent I had dealt with already had this property on her books. I had even mentioned it to her, but she seemed determined to steer me toward the more expensive properties. When I told her I was going to inspect it, she said she didn't recommend it because it had no natural light—in her words, 'It's a cave.'

But natural light wasn't a key factor for me, because with natural light comes street noise. I wanted to build a recording studio and a film studio, so I was willing to trade off natural light for silence. But she didn't ask me what I wanted and how I was going to use my office, so she never understood my needs. She missed a vital clue that would have led to a sure sale.

When a sale occurs, the order taker often has no idea how it happens. They fly blind, never realising that understanding what is right for their clients is crucial to a sale and a happy client. Their sales are mostly flukes.

Sales should never be a game of Pin the Tail on the Donkey. Take off the blindfold and ask questions. Develop a deeper understanding of your clients' needs and you will make more sales.

Discover their real motivation

Salespeople often talk about the need to discover a property seller's motivation. 'No motivation, no sale,' many say. This is true, but many salespeople don't understand what motivation really means, and therefore don't know how to question their sellers deeply enough to discover their true motivation.

Everyone is already motivated; the question is 'By what?' Your job is to discover what motivates your prospects and then show them how you can help them. Only then will they buy.

There is one little word in that paragraph many salespeople miss: *what*.

For example, a seller says, 'We're selling because we're moving to Brisbane,' so the salesperson thinks moving to Brisbane is the motivation. But all the salesperson knows is *where* the seller wants to go. *Where* isn't the same as *what*. The salesperson still doesn't know the seller's true motivation, but may think he or she does. This is dangerous.

You can work hard to sell a property, only to have the sellers change their mind because their reasons for staying are more compelling than those for selling. All that work for no result! And all because the salesperson didn't discover the sellers' true motive.

The problem begins with the words *motive* and *motivation*. These terms are common in sales training, but they are sterile words that disguise the first thing a salesperson must discover: *What is their real reason for selling?*

Let's remove *motivation* altogether and ask this:

How will the sellers' lives improve as a result of this move?

This is a much better question, because it reveals the benefits in moving. Ask this and you will find the *what* instead of the *where*.

Using our earlier example of the sellers moving to Brisbane, how will their lives improve after they make this move? Ask the question, and take time to uncover what motivates them. Help them clarify and express their goal.

For example, they may say they used to live in Brisbane, but moved because of a job opportunity. But after moving they found it difficult because they didn't know anyone in the new area. They couldn't go out at night very often because they didn't have anyone to look after the children; they had no friends and no support base.

Now you are getting to the emotional issues: loneliness, isolation and a lack of support. Their motivation is to be back among family and friends, and their lives will improve when they achieve that.

When you know the emotional reasons, you know *what* motivates them. At the time of listing, this might not seem important, but it is. When you list sellers, is it important for your integrity that you do so only if it is right for them to sell? Before I ever listed anyone, I wanted to know whether they should sell or not, because I believe you shouldn't convince anyone to do anything that isn't right for them.

After the property is listed, knowing the *what* is even more important. For example, if they decline a fair offer because they believe it is $10 000 too low, you can use their emotional reason for selling to offset the $10 000:

'You told me you are lonely, that you cannot wait to move to Brisbane—is that correct? So why are you saying no to something so important to you, your family and your wellbeing? We all know this offer is fair. Saying no to it will mean you stay here, and remain lonely, without the support of the people you love.'

You can see there is far more to this than merely a move to Brisbane. It is that 'far more' you need to uncover.

Motivation is elusive, but if you ask the right questions you will find the real reasons—the emotional reasons.

Motivation does not just apply to real estate. It is an important factor in all types of decision making—whether it's getting a teenager to clean her room, persuading a colleague to share information with you, or selling any kind of product or service. No motivation, no result.

Beware of false assumptions

There's an old saying: 'One person's gain is another's loss.' This is often totally untrue. Happiness is relative, and what pleases one person might not please the next. Two people with different values can negotiate an outcome that will suit both of them. Neither has to triumph at the expense of the other.

In *The Secret of Selling Anything*, Harry Browne says, 'What makes me happy may not make you happy. It is knowledge of the relative nature of happiness that enables us to facilitate negotiations where everybody leaves the table satisfied.'

Salespeople who second-guess their clients give a presentation based on their own assumptions, and subsequently lose the sale.

You will never know what your clients want or will accept unless you ask the right questions. Build an understanding of what will make your clients happy.

Many salespeople won't invest the time and ask enough good questions to determine what it will take to win the business.

False assumptions send you down the wrong path. It's acceptable to make assumptions, as long as you test those assumptions as soon as possible.

Many years ago, we listed a property with too many tenants for its size. I conducted a buyer inspection and all was going well. We made our way through the various rooms, but then we came to the kitchen. I guided the buyers in ... at the precise moment that a tenant slammed a meat cleaver through a chicken's neck, beheading it in one stroke. The room looked like a crime scene.

Of course, the tenant didn't bat an eyelid, but I assure you the buyers did. Without skipping a beat, I said to them, 'I don't think this is the right property for you.' They agreed and we quickly left.

Not long after that inspection, the property sold. It sold for two reasons:

- The purchasers were prepared to renovate, which included tiling the kitchen, so the blood-soaked timber was no problem.
- The property was priced correctly for its present condition and for the current market.

Many people, including agents, described this property as a 'dog box', but someone was prepared to buy it under the right conditions.

So before you create objections for yourself because you think a property is terrible and will never sell, or because you think you know what your clients want and then present based on false assumptions, or because you believe that the clients will never accept the proposal you are about to make, remember that happiness is relative.

You might not know them as well as you think you do, and what makes you happy isn't necessarily what will make them happy.

Ask the right questions. Find out what their vision of 'happy' is, and then talk your way into a sale, not out of one.

Search for new business

If you're in Sales, you're in the business of looking for new business. If you don't do this every working day, you'll never win.

Shannon Goodson and George Dudley, in *The Psychology of Sales Call Reluctance*, propose, 'Though far from perfect, the relationship between call reluctance and sales performance is more predictable than the daily fluctuations in the Dow Jones average or weather forecast three days into the future.

That is, a salesperson who won't prospect is guaranteed to be a failure.'

My first lesson in Sales was that professional salespeople search for new business every working day. Salespeople prospect; order takers sit and wait, I was told. Prospect or perish.

The best salespeople know that to expect their company to provide them with all their leads makes them order takers, not winners. They know that for the winner, prospecting is always a major task. They may not enjoy doing it, but they recognise it has to be done, and on a scale that will make a difference. So they get on and do it.

In these days of over-the-top political correctness, too many people pussyfoot around and don't say what they mean. So let's tell it like it is: The wrong people give leaders the headaches. To those people I say: *Go hard, or go home.*

Come up with all the excuses you like, but if you won't go out and meet people — that is, find *new customers* for your company — you should leave. Clear the way for someone who isn't scared to take on this work.

Business is primarily about doing two things right: Finding new customers and keeping the customers you have.

If you are in real estate and don't get more than eight listings and four sales consistently each month, you aren't speaking to enough people.

The minimum activity levels over a five-day week are:

- prospecting calls (speaking to potential sellers): 200 people

- listing presentations attended: 5

- buyer property inspections: 8 to 10 (that's the number of property inspections, not buyer appointments; show one buyer five properties and you have completed five buyer property inspections)

- seller visits: 5

- substantial price reductions (reduced sufficiently to get the property sold; and depending on the number of listings you hold and the type of market you are in): 4.

Fall below this level and you aren't working hard enough on the right actions.

For the wrong people, the Do Not Call Register introduced in Australia some years ago is a godsend. Telephone prospecting is now more difficult, but the last time I checked there is still no Do Not *Door Knock* Register. And until there is, you can knock on doors until your knuckles bleed without fear of prosecution.

Too scared? Face your fear, or leave. Too lazy? Get to work, or leave. Too busy? Are you listing at least eight and selling at least four properties a month? If not, you are too busy doing the *wrong actions*. Start doing winning actions, and enjoy great results.

Get to work!

Make it a routine

Have you ever put off something you thought would be difficult? You dreaded starting but eventually you did it, only to find it was much easier than you expected. You couldn't imagine why you thought it would be so hard.

Prospecting is like that. It's not that difficult. All you have to do is start, then keep going, and it will soon become a winning habit.

There are only four reasons why salespeople don't prospect: They're scared, they're stupid, they're lazy, or they're rich.

When selling any product or service, prospecting is a *high persistence* job. Always prospect with a clear purpose and mission. For example, if you are selling real estate, before you pick up the telephone, or knock on your first door for the day, think:

- 'Who wants to sell?'
- 'Which property can I list today?'

And make it a game:

- 'I will find a listing today by midday!'

You don't need a library of scripts either. You can always use Bill Nasby's question, 'I'm a real estate agent looking for work. When are you planning on moving?' Smile as you say this and you will be pleasantly surprised at the responses you receive. Bill Nasby has a great prospecting program called *Doors to Success*, available at BillNasby.com.

Talk about a new listing that has recently come onto the market, 'Do you know anyone who might be interested in moving into this street?' Before you leave or put down the phone, ask, 'When are you planning on moving?' It's just not that difficult.

To be effective, I recommend you speak to 40 people each day. This is 200 per week and will give you two listings per week, or eight per month if you keep at it.

If you don't see immediate results, don't blame prospecting. Perhaps you've hit a vein of non-prospects. It happens. Persist.

One of my own rules for prospecting was to completely prospect each street. Speak to everyone in that street, even if it means some detective work. Often those who aren't at home are the sellers.

Get into the habit of asking the people you meet if they know anyone who is selling. This habit will set you up for life.

Adam Horth uses this question with past clients: 'Is there anything I can help you with at the moment?' He explains, 'It is an open question. When you say, "help you with anything", and you are referring to real estate, they're going to answer that question by talking about real estate. They might talk about renovations they're considering, their plans to buy, or their plans for selling or investing. Then you take the conversation from there.

'There are always things that happen in people's lives. They're not just sitting around their lounge watching TV. You want to come across a person who says, "Yes we are thinking about selling." And if you go about that with an interesting and non-threatening approach, you're not going to annoy people.'

If you want them to be interested in you, *you* must be interested in them. Interested people are interesting. When prospecting, don't just 'crunch the numbers', but make each conversation as interesting as possible.

More from Adam: 'As far as I'm concerned, the numbers are the most important thing. However, there is no point in doing the numbers if you are just after a yes or no answer. You have to look for the clues in things people say, such as, "We're staying here until the baby is born". You ask when the baby is due and if they're looking to upgrade after the baby is born. Investigate all clues.'

Again, prospecting does not just apply to real estate. Whatever you are selling, if you engage a healthy number of people in interesting conversations every day, you will make more sales. And because you regularly do it, prospecting ceases to be a chore. Make it a chore and you will dread doing it, avoid it and wallow in mediocrity.

Knock on doors

People who say door knocking is dead either haven't knocked on many doors or have a terrible door-knocking presentation. For such people, door knocking *is* dead. For the rest, it's alive and well.

A salesperson with the prospecting habit is rare. Adam Horth was determined to be the best he could be, so he learned the skill of prospecting from his earliest days in real estate. It's a skill that has paid dividends throughout his career.

In chapter 1, I mentioned Adam's results as a prospector; these results continued when he entered Sales. Adam's prospecting ability helped him become a winning salesperson very quickly. In his first year as a salesperson, he produced over $475 000 in fees. From there Adam grew to be one of the best salespeople in the industry. Today he is the principal of his own agency, working with the two leaders who gave him his start in real estate.

In August 2012, Adam opened his real estate office in Ipswich, Queensland, and needed listings. He listed 35 properties that month, 14 of which came from door knocking. Winning habits and skills are always there when you need them.

Meet as many people as possible in person and you will create memorable impressions on many people. These people will become a pipeline of business for you.

These days everyone raves about social media, but it has its limitations. I see agents spending many hours playing with Facebook and Twitter, when they should be out knocking on doors.

As Adam Horth says, 'Face to face, *not* face to Facebook.'

Try this: Go out and knock on 1000 doors. Ask the Bill Nasby question, 'Thanks for your time. I'm a real estate agent looking for work. When are you planning on moving?' Do that, and then tell me if door knocking isn't effective.

Overcome fear

In *Coaching Salespeople into Sales Champions*, Keith Rosen explains:

> *Most of us spend more time focusing on what we fear than on the goals or dreams we want to create.*

Let's face it: We're all pretty good at articulating what we don't want to happen in our lives, yet fall short when trying to come up with a vivid picture of what we do want, our goals and dreams. If you know what you don't want yet don't know what you do want, then where do you think you are going to continually be directing your thoughts and energy? Your goals and dreams don't even stand a chance.

In *Crunch Point*, Brian Tracy writes, 'In business the greatest fear—after the fears of firing someone or of being fired and of financial loss or bankruptcy—is the fear of confrontation. Often this confrontation doesn't mean an argument with somebody face to face, it is fear of confrontation with ourselves.'

Forcing yourself to do things you don't want to do, admitting to yourself that you're unmotivated, acknowledging that you're being lazy and that it's time for you to act, is also confrontation. It is personal confrontation, and some people don't want to do that either. They'd rather be in denial than face reality.

Tracy goes on, 'Identify some person, situation or action you fear and resolve to confront it immediately and get it behind you.'

That brings me right back to that client you didn't want to call: Place that call early, get it out of the way, and you'll feel good about yourself. That is how you overcome fear.

Brian Tracy uses the acronym SCAMM to describe actions, excuses or beliefs you hide behind to justify your circumstances, behaviour and performance:

- *Stories*: You tell yourself stories that aren't true. They go something like this: *You're a loser, no-one in your family has ever done it, so what makes you think you're any better than them?* Those are the destructive stories you tell yourself.

(continued)

- *Cons*: Cons are the things you fall for. Your parents taught you it's rude to pry, so as a salesperson you're afraid to ask the kinds of questions to get the answers you need so you can recommend the right solution for your clients.
- *Assumptions*: You make false assumptions and act on them instead of testing them.
- *Meaning*: You believe situations are worse than they really are.
- *Mindset*: The mindset of 'poor me': *I've got low self-esteem and I had a really hard childhood.* It's a victim mindset and if you suffer from that, read Dr Wayne Dyer's *Pulling Your Own Strings*, an excellent book on taking control of yourself and not allowing people to victimise you.

So don't SCAMM yourself!

You've been trained, so if you don't act there's a reason. Find the reason and fix the problem, or get out of Sales.

In *The Psychology of Sales Call Reluctance*, George Dudley and Shannon Goodson talk about process definition: 'Conditions are necessary for call reluctance to occur. A fever could mean you have the flu, it could also mean you have something else. Low prospecting activity could mean you have call reluctance but it doesn't mean you do. Three essential conditions— motivation, goals and goal-obstructing feelings—must be present before you can conclude you have authentic call reluctance.'

If prospecting activity is low and one of these conditions is missing, you're a call reluctance imposter. It is very important to tell one from the other.

The authors talk about debunking a call reluctance myth: 'The process definition of call reluctance firmly establishes that no salesperson, male or female, could be call reluctant unless they're both motivated and committed.'

You cannot be reluctant to achieve something you didn't want in the first place. Imposters don't care if they don't meet their prospecting goals, but salespeople with authentic call reluctance care very much. Imagine the pain and energy required to consistently prospect regardless of constant stress.

What keeps these salespeople going if it isn't motivation and commitment? It's certainly not job satisfaction. Salespeople with authentic call reluctance hang in as long as they can, usually until the system expels them. Imposters leave soon after their first confrontation with sales management.

Sales managers try to attract motivated and committed salespeople, yet they've probably had them all along. Some of their salespeople may have been suffering from call reluctance. Sales managers try to train their salespeople so they can't be accused of not caring. Management must learn to separate the genuinely call reluctant from those with low motivation and a poor work ethic.

Talk to people

I saw an advertisement for a new software product that promised: 'Never Deal with a Tenant or Buyer Enquiry Ever Again'.

I was speechless. Was this a joke? How could anyone think removing a reason for salespeople to contact clients is a good idea? Is talking to clients now beneath us?

Like it or not, your *number one* job is to talk to people. It's what you are well paid to do. Ignore that job and you are negligent in your duty.

The company in question was serious. And no doubt some real estate people will think it's a good idea. I know this because I once conducted a survey of 300 salespeople and asked, 'What jobs waste most of your time?' The results were eye-opening. Here are three of the top five:

- number 1: answering enquiry
- number 3: buyers
- number 5: following up.

This gave me a snapshot of the way many salespeople think—three of the top five were jobs salespeople are paid to do. All three involve talking to people, but they thought it was a waste of time.

High touch beats high tech every time.

I like technology as much as the next person and I consider myself an early adopter. But it's easy to become so occupied with the new that you take your eye off the basics.

Given the choice between something personal (such as a call or personal visit) and something impersonal (such as letters, SMS or email), *human contact is preferable.*

Never miss an opportunity to talk with clients, especially face to face. You can send letters and emails, or leave a message on voice mail, but always with the purpose of making personal contact.

Talk to people. It's what you're paid to do.

Leave high-tech gadgets that shield salespeople from their clients to those who think they're far too important to be interrupted.

I have seen salespeople focus so much on a social media campaign that they become distracted from talking to people. You might argue they're talking to people via social media. But do you consider sending texts or emails, or posting on social media sites, *talking* to people? I don't, and I know winners will agree with me.

My friend Nathan Brett, from Real Estate Dynamics, says, 'If an email runs for longer than a paragraph, *pick up the phone.*' That is sound advice.

In case you think I'm a dinosaur for recommending that salespeople be more involved in door knocking than social media, consider the return on investment. Salespeople often spend too much time on Facebook, Twitter and Instagram when they should be making calls. Many of these salespeople have very few 'friends' or followers. So their posts aren't viewed by enough people to generate business.

How many responses would you expect from 40 prospecting letters or from a tweeted message to 40 followers? Very few. But 40 conversations with potential home sellers? You never know where those conversations will lead.

Social media is best left to agency management. Agencies should have a profile on social media, while the primary duty of salespeople is to speak with people on the phone or in person.

Embrace change, but not at the cost of the basics.

Selling has always been about relationships. To be successful, you need to build relationships through a *series* of meaningful contacts.

Those always searching for the new don't like this advice. They would rather hide behind technology so they don't have to prospect.

Do you want to know the ultimate secret of social media? Get a meaningful message to as many people as you possibly can as often as you can. The ultimate social strategy? A set of knuckles applied to the outside of a door.

Never let your search for the latest technology, or the latest real estate tool, distract you from the most basic of essential actions—talk to people and win.

Tell the truth

Client care. Many salespeople use these words often, but their actions speak louder than words.

Over and above service, client care means giving clients the right advice, whether or not it is in your best interests to do so. It means always telling the truth to clients, never distorting it or omitting certain elements in order to persuade.

Telling the truth means telling the hard truths.

Salespeople often forget this. Many prefer to tell only the 'happy truths':

- 'The buyers liked the property.'
- 'The buyers thought the décor was lovely.'

But they avoid the hard truths:

- 'The buyers thought the property was too small for the price.'
- 'The buyers felt the property was $25 000 overpriced.'

Sellers need to know their property is overpriced based on buyer feedback. This will help them understand what their property is worth in the current market. Without facts they cannot make intelligent decisions.

Salespeople avoid delivering hard truths to sellers because they don't want to risk the sellers' displeasure. It's the fear of rejection.

Imagine if surgeons felt the same way—too scared to tell patients that radical surgery was the only option. Surgeons like this would do more harm than good.

Similarly, salespeople who are too scared to tell clients the whole truth, including the hard truths, do more harm than good. Clients expect you to communicate every aspect of their sale to them. If buyers aren't positive, or if the property is overpriced, you must tell your client.

If you are a 'people pleaser' you won't make it in Sales. These people avoid any chance of conflict by only telling others what they want to hear.

For people of integrity, there can be no other way but to tell the entire truth.

Show courtesy

Salespeople who treat buyers in a blasé manner should remember that those buyers will become sellers one day, and they will remember the agents who treated them well when they were purchasers.

Although no salesperson will admit to treating people badly, it happens often.

Some time ago I bid at auctions for my niece and her husband. Based on advice from agents, who told my niece that they were 'in the ballpark', they paid for reports on two separate properties. The bidding on both properties started higher than their budgets — we never got a bid in. In each case the agent had led them to believe they had a good chance of securing the property, and it cost them $2000 in reports they had no hope of using. They used my niece and her husband as under-bidders to stimulate the auction.

Both agents blamed the 'hot market' when my niece couldn't secure either property. When the agents claimed they had no idea these buyers were out of the market on their budget, they were either lying or incompetent.

Today my niece and her husband are homeowners and have upgraded since their original purchase. Guess which two agents were not invited to do a listing presentation?

Clients aren't a limitless resource. It is foolish to treat people as though there are plenty of others to take their place. Treat clients well and it will pay dividends, in job satisfaction and in results.

Geoff Burch, in *Writing on the Wall*, suggests that before you say no to a client, or treat them with indifference, imagine them standing in front of you with a purse full of money they want to give to you. Buyers and sellers want to give you their money. All you have to do is find out what they want and help them get it, and they will gladly hand you their money.

Agents who are too busy to return calls, or too important to arrive at the appointment on time, and those who aren't honest with buyers and sellers, have no long-term future in real estate.

Give all clients your time, attention and courtesy — whether or not you have any chance of doing business with them. Courtesy costs nothing but rewards well in the long term.

Negotiate

Negotiation has been called 'The Game of Life' because everything in your life revolves around it.

In *Negotiating Effectively within Your Own Organization*, Chester Karrass writes:

> *We are all negotiators. Knowing how to do it well is important. Good negotiators, those able to settle difficult problems and differences amicably, are recognised and respected. They're better able to cut through discord by finding a path to shared benefits. Ben Franklin remarks in his autobiography that those who avoid being confrontational will be received with a "readier reception and less contradiction" to their views.*

To settle difficult problems and differences amicably, and to share in the benefits, hold open conversation between all parties involved. As Karrass says, 'This can be difficult to achieve when emotion permeates the negotiation. With emotion come ego, anger, defensiveness, turf protection, and similar negative issues that can block a negotiation.' Things you did or said in rash moments can come back to haunt you. The same applies in business: If you upset clients, they will tell everyone they can about their bad experience.

Successful dialogue keeps communication channels open. It also means knowing when to keep quiet to avoid confrontation and objections. Silence is better than upsetting the other side with a statement you cannot retract.

Don't act rashly

If you are annoyed with someone, think of the damage an ill-worded email, phone call or social media message can cause. The message and damage control will tarnish your reputation, something you cannot afford. If you feel strongly enough to write something down, wait at least three hours before sending it. By then you will have cooled off and you can review the message objectively, and decide whether it might cause damage.

To win in the Game of Life, treat everyone with respect. Whether in a business or a family negotiation, treat the other parties with respect, don't speak in anger, show you are listening and, when it is your turn to speak, say what needs to be said.

Before you speak, be mindful of this:

'Say what you mean, mean what you say, but don't say it mean.'

Be firm if you have to, and always be frank, diplomatic, polite and kind. Treat others as you would like to be treated.

The older I get the more I appreciate the value of knowing when not to speak. I can think of many times I wish I had not said what I did, and there are times when I regret not saying what I later realised I should have said. But I usually don't regret remaining silent, biding my time and saying what needs to be said when the emotion is right, and when the other party is ready to communicate.

Respect their privacy

I recently saw a press release about a 'new eBay-style platform that allows vendors to bypass agents'. The service was designed to deliver transparency and allow vendors to avoid paying agents' fees. Sounds fair enough. I don't mind competition, and I especially respect good competition.

The founder of the service said one of the great frustrations for vendors and buyers was the lack of transparency around the sales process. Their solution was a 'vendor assisted' platform that *allows buyers to see what other buyers are offering*.

From a negotiating perspective, this is flawed. No negotiation expert will tell you it is smart negotiating to allow one buyer to hear what another has offered. What one buyer offers is *nobody's business* except the seller's (and the agent's, if one is involved).

Buyers at auction can hear what another buyer has offered, so they offer a small amount above the other buyer's offer. They don't offer the maximum price they're prepared to pay for the property; they offer $5000 or $1000 (or sometimes as little as $500) more than the other buyer.

Experts say that if you want to get a high price for anything, start high and reduce it until you find a buyer. They also say that offers should be given in confidence, without other parties being privy to them.

This new service offers transparency, but at the expense of privacy. If I give you an offer, I expect privacy. I expect you to pass it on to the seller, who considers it and then accepts or rejects it, or perhaps makes a counter-offer asking for more money.

I don't expect you to inform other interested buyers and play me off against them. Nor do I believe that passing my offer along to other buyers—as 'transparent' as it may be—is anything other than clueless negotiating on behalf of sellers who expect to get the *highest price* (which is different from a *high price*) for their property.

It is bad negotiation to allow one buyer to know what another will pay. Worse than that, it's a breach of privacy.

Look at what happens on eBay: Many buyers wait until the dying moments of the auction and then put in a last-second bid slightly higher than the current highest displayed offer. They win, but the seller doesn't get the highest price that buyer was prepared to pay. And there can be a massive difference between 'high' and 'highest'.

Every time I attend an auction, I say to the successful bidder, 'Congratulations, you must be happy. Tell me, would you have paid more?' Most say they would. If money is left on the table, that method of sale has let the seller down.

As a seller, I'll take privacy over transparency any day.

Close the sale

Closing has received a lot of bad press over the years. Many view closing as adversarial, thinking that if the closer 'wins', by default they have defeated the other person.

Closing isn't a fight with one winner. It is the simple act of helping somebody make a decision. It ties down the agreement so neither party has to revisit resolved issues. If someone agrees with you, they're closer to making a decision; they haven't lost a fight.

Closing isn't the final act of placing the pen into the hand of your prospect. Before the final close, there is much to do if you are to get an agreement and have a happy client.

As a professional salesperson, you must ensure that whenever you close, *it is right for the client.* To close someone on something that isn't in their best interest is incompetent, irresponsible and unprofessional.

This means you have a responsibility to care enough to uncover client need. This must always come before the close.

Find out the decision the client needs to make to solve their problem. Help them understand the actual problem and how to solve it. Then you can present the right solution. After you present the solution, and they agree to it, *then* you close.

Both of you win: The client has agreed to the solution that is right for them and you have made a sale. Close correctly, and on the right things, and everybody wins.

Here is the Closer's Formula:

- Uncover client needs.
- Get the client to *agree* this is a problem for them—one to which they would like solutions.
- Show your solutions to the problem.
- Have the client *agree* that these are suitable solutions.
- Close.

Get the order right, take time and show care, and it is difficult for the prospect to say no.

Care about the client and only close on things to which they should agree. That way they will never feel as though they were pushed into anything.

As you can see, there is a lot to do before you close, but put the client first, care about them and they will trust you; close responsibly and you do them a great service. Look after them and they will refer you to their friends and family.

Practise

Gary Ryan Blair writes in *Everything Counts*:

> *High achievers turn over all stones, understanding and exploiting to their benefit the fact that the critical distinction between merely acceptable versus excellent results lies in the smallest of details. They acknowledge and accept that the difference between gold and silver at the Olympics can be traced to the tiniest of differences in training or execution; as a result, they make everything count.*

Ask yourself, 'Can I do something else to get myself closer to my goal?'

If you don't practise, you'll take shortcuts. You might still get the listing signed, but you'll have trouble getting offers accepted or getting price reductions.

Keep trying things. You'll close badly before you ever learn to close well. You'll negotiate poorly before you ever learn to negotiate successfully. But if you deny yourself the practice, you'll deny yourself the perfection. If you don't like rejection, then how do you reduce the incidence of rejection? Practice, that's all. Get a lot of no's, then you'll start to get good at getting yeses. But if you don't practise, you'll just get used to rejection, and eventually give up and leave Sales.

Study for understanding

I introduced Sandy Rogers at the start of the book. After more than 15 years in Sales, Sandy is a stayer, and I interviewed her to discover the secret to her longevity in the profession.

A single mum with a young child at the time, Sandy had no support network when she started out; if her son wasn't with her, he was in day care. She needed to learn how to get results and still find time to spend with her son.

Sandy happily admits she made a lot of mistakes in her early years. But one mistake she didn't make was to shun training. Remember her words: 'I pulled the manual apart.'

Before reaching this point, Sandy merely *read* her manual. She could recite her sales scripts word for word, but she didn't understand them. It's only when she truly understood the intent behind them that she started to succeed.

Every time clients ask a question such as 'Why should I list with you?', you are being tested. The only way you will know what to say is to understand what you are being asked so you can form the right reply. You do this through study.

This does not just apply to real estate. Clients test salespeople all the time. They do so by raising objections. How you respond to those objections marks the difference between success and failure.

Studying will give you the right words to say, but it's understanding that guides you toward using the right words effectively. Even a change of tone can change the meaning of what you say. Understanding guides you on the tone and body language to use. Understanding, with the right words, the right timing and the right tone, leads to the right *delivery*.

Many salespeople stay at the level where they can recite the right words. Few study their craft to the level of understanding. These people are the winners.

There are many subtle nuances in Sales. In the early days Sandy wasn't *connecting* with people and didn't really understand them. She launched into her presentation too soon, before she fully understood what was important to the client.

If you don't know what is important to your clients, you cover everything in your presentation, which makes it too long and largely irrelevant.

By studying for understanding, Sandy learned not to rush into her presentation. She would first find out what was important to clients and then target the presentation toward showing them how, by appointing her, they would get what was important to them. This was the turning point in Sandy's career.

American sales trainer Tom Hopkins presses this point often: Practise, Drill and Rehearse.

This is the essence of studying for understanding. It means getting the words into your head, practising the delivery of those words in regular role-plays—the 'drill' part—and rehearsing constantly.

In client presentations, you often have to think on your feet. Sometimes you have to take your presentation in a different direction based on what your client has just said. People new to Sales can't think on their feet because they know the words but lack the finesse that comes with understanding. Prepared people think on their feet.

Handle every objection

If you want the right words to come out of your mouth at the right time, the right words must be in your head in the first place. Study for understanding and you will be able to handle every objection that comes at you. You will say the right things at the right time, pause at the right time, ask the right questions and close at the right time. And you will do this unconsciously.

Sales is a wonderful profession, one that deserves far more care and attention than most salespeople give it.

You've got to be good to survive in Sales in the long term. Just as Sandy Rogers did, you must study for understanding.

Summary

In my experience, all the skills described in this chapter are essential for consistent, reliable long-term success. I recommend that you assess your skills by asking yourself these questions:

- Are there some skills I already use well? If so, what can I learn to do even better—even if it's only a *bit* better?

- Are there some skills I must improve? (Start to work on them now!)

- Are there some skills I don't believe are essential? (I invite you to challenge yourself and reconsider.)

- Are there some skills I think *someone else I know needs to learn?* (Often this is a sign that *you* need to learn it as well, because we often see in others things we don't see in ourselves.)

What's next?

Now you have the skills, let's put them into practice. The next step in your four-step success journey is to take competent action.

COMPETENT ACTION

Bill, another salesperson I admired, was extremely successful. Over time, he had become unconsciously competent—he was what many people call a 'natural' salesperson.

Bill would come to the office early and either do photocopier demonstrations in the showroom or go out to service his territory. He was happy to work late into the night helping newcomers like me, but it had to be outside normal business hours, because daylight hours were for selling.

I was privileged to spend a lot of time with Bill, especially after I was given a new, more challenging territory.

Photocopier technology was changing rapidly around that time. We worked on commission only, and if we sold a machine over the minimum price set by the marketing department, we split the 'overs' 50/50 with the company. So if a machine had a set minimum of $10 000 and I sold it for $12 000, I earned $1000 and $1000 went to the company.

One of our biggest competitors marketed a copier that caused me the most trouble. It was a heavily featured machine that retailed for $3000 less than the minimum price of our equivalent model. One day I asked Bill how he managed to sell our copier for $18 000—way over our set minimum, and far more than the competitor's machine.

(continued)

Bill gave me a lesson in selling that went something like this:

- He asked me how much a secretary was paid. When I was slow to answer this seemingly random question, he replied, 'They earn 18 cents a minute.'

- He then asked me what I saw when I looked at the dashboard of the competitor's copier. I said, 'It's got a lot of features,' to which he replied, 'Features mean buttons. The more buttons, the more complicated the dashboard. Would you agree?' I would.

- Next Bill asked, 'Would it be reasonable to suggest that a secretary could spend two minutes standing at the machine thinking about which buttons to press?' I agreed, and he continued, 'This means you can add 36 cents to the cost of the copy the secretary just made.'

- Next came the master class. Bill said he found it best to increase the price of our machine to a figure far above that being charged by our competitor. 'By taking it to a much higher price point, I can argue that our machine is a high-quality workhorse for people who want simplicity and high volume. The saving of 18 cents per minute of secretaries' time means my clients would pay back the higher price over time through labour savings. (Of course, over time regular users will become quicker at operating the equipment, but there can be no argument that the more complicated the dashboard, the longer initial setup takes before the first copy is produced.)

Not long after that discussion I sold one of our machines for $18 000! Bill was extremely happy for me and stood with me when I wrote the sale up on the board.

I learned many valuable lessons that day, the most important being never to compete on price—value for money is what clients want.

Bill was rich even then. He bought and sold real estate and had built an extensive investment portfolio. Eventually he bought the company. He had used Sales as the vehicle to his success.

Bill was a hard worker, knew his products and was always willing to give back by spending time with new people. There's no question Bill was a winner.

What's the point?

Before my discussion with Bill, although I was working hard, most of my actions were incompetent. Most businesses don't have training problems; they have *action* problems. Generally, their salespeople have problems performing the right actions competently, and in sufficient quantities.

This chapter is about taking action — *competent* action.

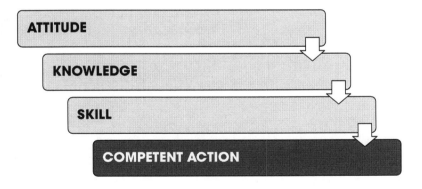

Some people believe that once they reach a certain level of competence, all their subsequent actions will also be competent. This isn't the case. Everyone can be 'off their game' occasionally, performing incompetently as a result. Even winners give lacklustre performances occasionally. Keep the focus on *competent*.

In practice, we often take incompetent action first, learn the skills to improve and then take competent action. If you practise the wrong actions, you'll be repeating incompetent actions. Competent action comes from gaining knowledge, trying it in the field, making mistakes, learning from those mistakes and trying again. It's all about practice: doing things badly before you do them well, and being willing to work at improvement.

Businesses implement training to ensure their staff have the necessary skills and knowledge. That training has to be put into action that produces results. No leader can afford to keep you if you don't produce results, so work hard on the right activities.

Waiting for business, or working hard on the wrong actions, is a career killer for people in any profession. You can attend courses and read books, but at some point you have to get to work, and to work hard on the right actions. It's your choice.

Focus every day

Keith Rosen writes in *Coaching Salespeople into Sales Champions*:

> *The most productive people master the art of abandonment: the ability to let go of old stuff that no longer works. We all want better results but in order to generate these desired results, we must do what precedes them: change. We have to change something first.*

You have to change yourself. Indeed, the only person you can control is yourself. So what's your focus? Decide, plan and get to work. And I mean *work*. When you're at work, work. Eliminate unfocused thoughts and actions. Work on what matters most.

Set daily actions

Successful people do more of the right actions every day over the long term. By 'right actions', I mean actions that lead to results. More of the right actions means more results, and more results lead to more success. Most people know the right actions but seem incapable of performing them consistently.

If you don't like to set goals, try another approach: Focus on doing the right actions for just one day.

Think of the actions you need to perform daily if you are to succeed as a real estate salesperson:

- prospecting for new business: a minimum of 40 potential sellers spoken with
- visiting your current listings: one seller, face to face, asking for a price reduction if necessary
- conducting four buyer property inspections
- attending the day's seller and buyer appointments.

If I asked you to do this every day, you might say it's impossible. But could you do it for just *one* day?

Suppose I kidnapped someone close to you and told you my ransom demand was that tomorrow you had to make 40 prospecting calls, visit one of your current sellers, conduct four buyer property inspections, and fit this extra activity around your day's seller and buyer appointments... or I would kill your loved one. Could you do it? Yes! Of course you could do it for just one day.

If you spend just one day doing the right actions and nothing else, you will prove to yourself you can do it. You will start to take control of your career, and it will be the start of something great.

Lao Tzu said, 'A journey of a thousand miles begins with a single step.' I say, 'A successful career begins with doing the right actions for just one day.'

Prove to yourself that:

- you know the right actions
- you can do the right amount of the right actions for a single day.

You will feel proud of yourself. You'll finish this one day knowing you gave nothing but your best, and you'll be inspired to try it again.

I hope you will find it addictive. High achievers are addicted to spending their days doing the right actions constantly. Try it.

Group your tasks

A few years ago, my wife bought four flat-pack wardrobes, which needed assembly. It took me about 45 minutes to assemble the first wardrobe. The second took around 35 minutes, the third around 25, and I finished the fourth in under 20 minutes. The more I repeated the same tasks, the quicker I got.

This is the advantage of grouping your tasks. The more you do the one type of task, the more efficient you become.

Rather than making one or two prospecting calls, a buyer appointment and a listing presentation, you will do better if you group similar tasks:

- Set aside a block of time and do nothing but prospect.
- Attend three listing presentations in a row.
- Organise two or three buyer appointments back to back.

Have you ever conducted three listing presentations in a row? By the time you reach the third appointment you are in 'listing mode'. If you knocked on the wrong door, you'd still list that homeowner, even if they said you were at the wrong house and they didn't want to sell!

Task hopping is time wasting. People delude themselves by saying they are multitasking. There is no such thing.

Try this: Take two sheets of paper and two pens. Hold one pen in your left hand and one in your right. With your non-writing hand write this simple sum: 4 + 6 + 8 = 18. *At the same time*, with your writing hand, write this sentence: 'The quick brown fox jumps over the lazy dog.'

I doubt you can do both at the same time. If you completed both, you probably wrote out the sum with one hand then wrote the sentence with the other, or you hopped from one task to the other until both were complete, but you didn't do both at the same time.

Dave Crenshaw discusses this common self-delusion in his book *The Myth of Multitasking*. People like to think they multitask, but they actually switch task, swapping from one to the other. This inefficient approach wastes many hours over a working week.

Wherever possible, I try to group similar tasks. I set aside blocks of time to write or to present at speaking engagements, for example.

You might say that as a salesperson, your time is at the mercy of other people. I've been there, making excuses about why I can't do something. You are the only one who controls what appointments are entered into your diary. You are in charge of you.

Exercise this control. Group your tasks, and do each block of tasks well.

Don't stack problems

My daughter and son-in-law were involved in putting out a small brush fire, started by a wayward sky rocket. I won't say who set it off, but for the record I wasn't within 100 kilometres. I would have used real rockets, just for starters!

The fire was extinguished in less than five minutes, but in that time it was interesting to see how 'Problem Stackers' quickly added to the difficulty of putting out the flames.

A Problem Stacker is someone who 'piles up' problems, or adds layers of difficulty to problem solving.

On this occasion, two Problem Stackers emerged. The first not only panicked but got in the way while she did so. This Problem Stacker was pushed out of the way so the Problem Solvers could get on with the job.

The second Problem Stacker was more interested in apportioning blame than putting out the fire. This prize idiot kept asking who set off the rocket, all the while yelling out, 'Don't you know how dangerous that is?' While this is true, this wasn't the time to state the obvious.

I won't say exactly what my son-in-law said to this Problem Stacker, but it was along the lines of 'Get some water or get [something else!]'.

Before they could do the job of putting out the fire, the Problem Solvers had to remove two Problem Stackers. Do you see the problem with problem stacking? It's a sure way to get nothing done, or at least to slow down a task or project.

There are two types of Problem Stackers:

- everybody else
- ourselves.

When the Problem Stackers are other people and you need to solve a problem, first identify them, then remove them by politely asking them to allow you to solve the problem. If it's your boss, be extra polite.

When the Problem Stacker is ourselves, it is more difficult. Problem stacking is neurotic behaviour, and it can be hard to identify such flaws and address them objectively.

We problem-stack for ourselves when we look at *all* the problems we face instead of dealing with them one at a time. Nobody can fix ten problems at once, but we can fix one problem at a time.

Work on one problem, fix it so it doesn't come back, then move to the next. It's much simpler, much less demotivating, and a sure way to work through life's challenges.

In *Fierce Conversations*, Susan Scott advises, 'Tackle your toughest challenge today. Burnout doesn't occur because we're solving problems; it occurs because we've been trying to solve the same problem over and over. The problem named is the problem solved. Identify and then confront the real obstacles in your path.'

Winners deal with their toughest challenges first.

When we stack our problems, we focus on how much there is to do and how hard it's going to be, then do nothing.

But when we take one challenge at a time, think about what we need to do to overcome the challenge, and then do it, we feel invigorated because we are accomplishing something.

For example, when I'm writing articles, it is easy to think of how many more articles I have to complete. But when I focus on the task at hand my attitude changes: I think that when I finish this article, it's one less to do; with every word I write, I am getting closer to crossing this task off my to-do list.

Focus on the *now*.

There's an old saying: 'How do you eat an elephant?' Answer: 'One bite at a time.' I apologise to vegetarians, and I'm not encouraging supermarkets to stock elephant steaks, but you get the point: Every task is accomplished piece by piece, and every set of problems is solved one by one.

Don't be a Problem Stacker. You'll get nothing done and it will rob you of the enjoyment of gratifying work.

Don't wait for tomorrow

What is a result? In real estate only four things count:

- an exclusive listing is obtained
- a sale is started
- one of your listings becomes saleable
- a sale becomes unconditional.

The best advice ever given to me as a fledgling salesperson was to strive for one result each working day. Learn to start working on this result as soon as you get into the office and keep working until it's achieved.

The salespeople who keep their careers this simple outperform those who arrive at the office each day wondering what task they will tackle first.

Get to the office; work for a result. Can time management get any simpler?

Now for the bad news.

Many salespeople begin their careers with the intention of obtaining a result each day, but before too long they fall victim to what I call 'the Tomorrow Principle'.

A salesperson who completes all appointments for the day with no result accepts this lack of progress with a reassuring 'I'll do better tomorrow'. Before you are tempted to write off a day without a result, think about how you could get just one result—even though you have no more appointments today.

You might not have any listing or buyer appointments left that day, but the following two tasks might still produce a result before you go home, or at least set you up for a result the next day.

- Make time to visit one of your sellers (vendors) in person. Talk with the sellers about what needs to be done to get their property sold. Talk about the price reduction you know they need. As long as you have listings, you can always get a result.

- Set up at least one listing appointment, one appointment with a qualified buyer, and one appointment with one of your sellers for tomorrow. If you set up good appointments, you will have a much better chance of getting a result.

You might still finish the day without a result, but if you don't give in to the Tomorrow Principle, you know you gave your best effort to getting a result. Today must be your focus.

Monitor your time

Low productivity is often blamed on things like alcohol, stress, lack of motivation and such, but for real estate agencies time is most often lost through salespeople not knowing what to do next. Some people believe time is lost in large chunks, but often this isn't true. Most time is lost minute by minute: a few minutes lost here, a few there, and these lost minutes add up to large blocks of time lost each day.

The greatest waste of time comes from poor-performing salespeople who steadfastly refuse to follow a plan. When moving to the next task, because they have no plan they do something that doesn't lead to a result.

I always believed myself to be a good time manager—until I read Alec Mackenzie's book *The Time Trap*. Mackenzie recommends keeping a time log to see how much time you spend on activities that specifically lead to results. 'To use your time more effectively,' he says, 'the essential first step is to discover what you currently do with it.'

When I conducted a time log, I discovered on the first day I invested a mere 30 per cent of my time in activities that led directly to results.

Think about this for a minute: I was doing a time log, so I was on my best behaviour, consciously aiming to devote a healthy percentage of time to completing important or urgent tasks by the end of the day, and yet the best I could manage was 30 per cent.

This exercise illustrated that without clearly defining what activities lead to results, and without putting together a simple plan that leads you toward those activities, you will waste a lot of time thinking about what needs to be done next.

What activities lead to results? Any activity in which you become personally involved with potential sellers, listed sellers and buyers.

There are some other important activities, such as goal setting, planning, attending sales meetings, and so on. But with the exception of attending sales meetings, these activities don't have to be done during daylight. The golden rule is not to perform a 'night time' task during daylight hours.

There are many time management tools, but none is more important than Alec Mackenzie's time log. It will identify where and how you are wasting your time, and it will teach you how to spend your time on the important activities that lead to Sales greatness.

Although I have told thousands of salespeople about *The Time Trap* (note: read the third edition or earlier; the fourth edition is a rewrite that doesn't contain the time log), too few actually follow through and complete 30-day time logs.

One benefit I always point out: If you currently spend 30 per cent of your day on activities that don't produce results, double that to 60 per cent, without working an extra minute, and you have just doubled your sales!

Salespeople who don't implement Mackenzie's advice drift through their careers, wasting time thinking about what needs to be done next. Instead, learn what needs to be done, plan to work mostly on those activities, and conduct a time log to ensure you maintain your focus on all those important activities.

Hard work and application

In grammar, there are nouns and verbs. A noun names a person, place, thing, quality or action. A verb is a doing word. But words can switch functions. Some nouns have morphed into verbs: For example, the noun *Google* is now also commonly used as a verb: we 'Google' things on the internet.

The real meaning of the verb *work* has been lost in its transition from verb to noun. We *do* work. We don't *go to* work. Yet this is how many people use the word. This confusion causes problems.

'Bye, darling, I'm off to work,' should instead be, 'Bye, darling, I'm off to the office.' And, once you arrive, you should *do* some work.

Many salespeople think that because they're dressed up and at the office, they're working. But if they are not speaking with clients, there is a chance they're not doing anything that leads to results. It *might* be work, but more likely it is self-delusion.

You are paid for results, not for hours worked, or for time spent at the office. So let's put the emphasis back on *doing* work.

Structure your day

One simple adjustment to your day could rocket you to success.

Statistics indicate that most salespeople don't begin working on results-producing activities until around 11 am each day. They might arrive at 9 am, but they don't start to work for two hours.

Imagine how much better your business life, and your income, would be if you restructured your day.

From 9 am to 1 pm focus on finding new business. Four hours a day (which includes those two 'lost' hours, wasted by so many salespeople) should be spent doing nothing else but speaking with potential clients.

It is a radical thought, but this simple daily routine puts the emphasis on finding new business, something too often pushed to the back of the priority queue when salespeople become busy ... with the wrong activities.

Agents complain about a shortage of listings. They say whatever they list, they sell. 'If only we could get more listings,' they fret. I say, 'Allocate more time to finding more listings.' This is the solution to the shortage of listings, but few make prospecting a priority, preferring instead to bemoan their lack of listings.

After 1 pm, attend to appointments and carry out all your other duties.

Success is a combination of attitude, knowledge, skill and *action*. The missing ingredients for many salespeople are *the correct actions performed competently*.

Try it. Don't *go* to work—*do* work. The right kind of work. Work that brings results.

Don't coast

People work in different ways and at different paces. It pays to know your personal work patterns. It is rare to find a person who can work steadily for eight hours a day. Energy levels rise and fall, and work concentration ebbs and flows with them.

Some people are 'sprinters': they do focused work for short periods then coast for a while. If this is your work pattern, don't beat yourself up; understand it and work with it. The trick is to ensure your 'on' periods of focused work produce results. If they don't, you need more work spurts!

Coasters, on the other hand, seldom sprint—they coast nearly all the time. This isn't a good thing. Coast for long enough and it can become an ingrained work ethic that leads to a mediocre career.

The younger you are, the more energy you have. Don't waste your prime earning years by coasting.

I love Mark McKeon's idea of having a 'Go Zone' every working day. For one hour per day, you do nothing else but focus on an activity that produces results, without any interruptions or excuses. Everyone is capable of doing that, but many who know about it choose not to do it.

How much could you achieve if you worked harder? I'm not suggesting you sacrifice your family for your career. Relationships aren't always under strain because one or the other partner is working too hard. Relationships are often under strain because of financial difficulty.

You can fix that. Work harder. Set goals, plan, follow your plans, save money, invest wisely, and set yourself and your family up financially as quickly as you can.

Jim Rohn says: 'The sooner you get money out of the way, the sooner you will be able to get to the rest of your problems in style.'

Don't coast through your play time either. Plan fun activities with your family and friends. Make the most of your life, including your leisure time.

Relationships can suffer through lack of communication. This means couples don't talk to each other. Turn off the TV. Do something fun with your partner that creates memories. Talk. Listen—this especially applies to men. Be together, not together in front of the TV.

Don't make a habit of coasting through life.

Exercise willpower

Willpower and stubbornness are closely related. One attribute you want, the other you don't.

Stubborn people steadfastly hold on to ideas, right or wrong, and won't be persuaded to see any other point of view. This is misdirected willpower.

When it comes to forming new habits, you need willpower. With willpower you can say yes or no to yourself and mean it.

If you feel you lack willpower, take heart. Willpower can be exercised. Start small. Make a short-term commitment and persevere. Increase the time and difficulty of the commitments over time, and your willpower will strengthen.

Promise yourself you will persist with this commitment and use your willpower to ensure you do. Don't accept any excuses from yourself. Don't wait for 'a better time'.

Never make resolutions; make commitments.

Keep trying, and don't aim for perfection.

Weight Watchers has a saying I love: 'If you eat more than you planned, don't wait until the next *day* to get back on track, start at the next *meal*.'

If you have a day when you don't perform your task, start again immediately. Don't give up — exercise your willpower. You don't have to be perfect.

Choose an item from this list and commit to it, then move on to another:

- Search for new listings. Make 25 good prospecting calls per day for 30 days.

- After 30 days increase the 25 prospecting calls to 40. Do this for 90 days.

- Write your goals 15 times each working day before 8.30 am. Do this for 90 days.

- Telephone four of your listed sellers each day (or if you are not in real estate sales, phone four of your best clients). Set one appointment per day. Do this for 30 days.

- Read a motivational or educational book for 30 minutes each day for 90 days.

- Start a new seller source (for example, 'For Sale by Owner') today, and do it for one month. If you are not in real estate, think, where can I find new clients?

- Set one good listing appointment for each working day for one month.

- Plan a Best Month Ever and follow through for one month.

- Send at least five thank-you notes per day for six months.

- Obtain one price reduction per day for 10 days.

- Eat a healthy, non-fattening breakfast every day.

- Save a percentage of everything you earn. Start at 5 per cent for six months.

- Attend one seminar per quarter.

- Set three alcohol-free days per week. If you have a problem doing this, you should call Alcoholics Anonymous (seriously).

- Do something uplifting with your spouse and kids each week for six months.

- Plan (and take) one good holiday and two shorter 'reward breaks' per year.

- Obtain one *real* result (a listing, a sale started, a substantial price reduction or an unconditional contract) per day each working day for one month.

- Enter 'Today's Forecast' into your diary at the start of each day, and 'Today's Results' at the end of each day for 12 months. On days when you didn't get a result, write 0. You can still do this with electronic diaries.

- Walk briskly for 20 minutes three days each week—rain, hail or shine. Do this for six months.

- Don't have your first cup of tea or coffee at the office until you have spoken to five clients — sellers, buyers or potential sellers.

- Call ten buyers daily and qualify them.

- Role-play your listing presentation once a week for 90 days.

- Do the hard tasks *first*. Do this every day for six months.

- Call a winner once a week, ask for their advice, set actions and carry them out. Do this for 12 months.

Exercise your willpower with these, or similar, exercises. There are many more you can add to the list. Anything is acceptable, as long as your life — professional, personal or spiritual — improves because you committed to it.

Be tough on yourself or life will be tough on you.

Create great habits

As important as it is to exercise willpower, there's something even more powerful: habit.

Habits are the foundation of success. As you progress through your sales career, your results will improve as you replace bad habits with good habits. A salesperson who operates at the mediocre level works much harder than one who works towards greatness. It's also much more stressful.

Your habits will make or break you.

Set goals

Winners don't 'wing it'. They set goals, carefully calculating what targets they need to achieve if they're to reach those goals.

Once they have their targets, winners formulate plans. They calculate how many potential sellers they need to speak with each working day, how many presentations they will attend, how many listings will come from those presentations, and how many of those listings will sell. They know how many price reductions they must achieve each month, and how many buyer appointments they need.

These are real estate examples, but every business has statistics that point to how and where clients can be found. Analyse the statistics for your business and formulate your plans to ensure that you boost your client contact—new and existing—to higher levels. Do that and you will make more sales.

Nothing is left to chance. Everything is carefully calculated and planned.

Winners know that actions without purpose are a waste of time.

Prospect heavily

Mediocre salespeople are too busy to prospect. Winners aren't.

Winners know they must work on listings to replace those that will inevitably sell. Incoming leads provided by the office won't be enough for them to reach their goals. Winners know they need to prospect.

Speak to 40 potential sellers every working day—200 a week—and your results will soar.

Communicate more with sellers

Winners stay in touch with their sellers, whether or not there have been inspections on their properties. Even if nothing is happening, that alone is something to talk about. When there has been no interest from buyers, winners visit the sellers and recommend a price reduction.

Mediocre salespeople play 'duck and hide'. They avoid their sellers, who then inevitably blame the salesperson for lack of interest. These salespeople don't realise it, but the sellers will list and sell with the next agent who takes over the property. Through their lack of care and courage, these mediocre salespeople are working for the opposition. They just don't know it.

Avoiding what must be done is never a good practice—in any industry or in your personal life. 'Duck and hide' always makes things worse. Be it a tough client, a tough decision, or simply a difficult situation that needs attention, *do it now*. Procrastination is a cowardly strategy.

Pay attention to price

If a property isn't selling, it's overpriced. Winners know it, but mediocre salespeople don't want to face this fact.

In any market, you will make sales if your listings are priced at or near *fair market price*. Mediocre salespeople don't know what fair market price is, so cannot recommend fair market prices to their sellers. They also don't want to risk their sellers' displeasure.

Winners know that if a listing is to sell, it must be fair value for the *current* market. Winners don't blame the market for lack of sales; they take responsibility for their results. They coach their sellers so they confidently reduce to the right price to sell.

Here is another strategy: *show value to justify your price*. This is difficult in real estate, because a property can only be styled so far before a large capital expenditure is required to improve its presentation further. But if you sell other products or services and if your prices are fixed, think of as many reasons as possible to justify your asking price. Think: value for money—what do we offer for what we charge? Build a list of client benefits and present them enthusiastically.

Work with qualified buyers

The sure sign of a desperate salesperson is one who works with a lot of unqualified buyers.

Winners work with a small number of qualified buyers and actively seek out properties that suit those buyers. They are active prospectors, and prospect where qualified buyers want to buy.

In Sales, the greatest time waster is spending too much time with the wrong people. It is a recipe for a disastrous career (actually, I think it's a recipe for a disastrous life).

Work with qualified buyers only. Show them properties priced to *sell*. You will make more sales, regardless of the market.

Learn constantly

Winners train. They know it takes as long to get a listing as it does to miss one, so why not train and do your best to turn every appointment into a result?

You never have to force a winner to train. Winners constantly look for ways to do things better.

Act differently

You may be able to think of more great habits. This is good—you are thinking. But thinking is only part of the equation. You also have to act.

Perhaps you have already instilled these habits into your work life. If not, think how much better you would be if you:

- had clear written goals and followed a clear plan every month
- spoke with a minimum of 40 potential sellers every working day

- communicated with your sellers instead of playing 'duck and hide'
- worked at pricing all of your listings at fair market price
- worked with qualified buyers only
- trained hard, constantly working toward excellence.

I know I've said this often, but these are critical elements to success. They are the habits of winners. I hope they're your habits too.

Be passionate about getting better

Sales can be a tough career. Most salespeople face rejection daily. They do most of their presenting in unfamiliar territory. They know they are only as good as their last order — and if they don't sell, they don't eat. Like everyone else, they have bills to pay. Days without results (most days for many salespeople) can be extremely stressful.

Selling isn't for everyone. In fact, many experts estimate 80 per cent of salespeople are in the wrong career. They lack the temperament for Sales.

What must life be like for the mediocre salesperson? Every day they must wonder whether this is the day they will be asked to leave. To them, rejection is hard to endure.

I knew one salesperson who was on the verge of bankruptcy. She had spent weeks putting together a sale with a potential fee of $16 000. She needed this money desperately. Everything was agreed. The buyer had signed and she only needed the owners' signatures.

The sale was nearly complete. But we know you cannot eat 'nearly'. At the eleventh hour, the owners said to the salesperson, 'We are sorry to put you to all this trouble, but we have decided not to sell.' The salesperson told me later it was all she could do not to burst into tears in front of those sellers. Desperate salespeople don't sell well, and I felt desperately sorry for her.

I've mentioned that 80 per cent of salespeople are in the wrong career. But I also believe many of these 'Eighty Percenters' could develop a temperament for Sales if only they would do things differently.

Stop doing the same things over and over again when you know they don't work. Stop doing things that don't work and start doing things that do.

Failing to do things properly adds to the stress of mediocre salespeople.

To be good at Sales you have to love it. But it's hard to love something you're not good at.

Do you want to enjoy your work? Do you want less stress? Here is a tip: Get good.

Talk tough to yourself

Many salespeople say things like this:

- 'I'll try harder tomorrow.'
- 'I'm tired — result or not, I'm going home!'

Most people need to be tougher on themselves and to expect more. They need to engage in regular, tough self-talk. Don't allow yourself to be convinced you cannot do what you want to do in life. When someone says, 'It's tough,' you say, 'Of course it's tough, but I choose to focus and not fold.'

Everyone can be successful. For some it's going to take more training, application and effort, but it can be done.

I am capable of deciding what I want from life. I can decide if I'm willing to pay the price and then work toward getting what I want. If I'm capable of doing this, so are you.

We get two possible outcomes in life: reasons or results. What are you getting? Do you make excuses, or do you quietly insist on achieving, focusing and getting what you want from your life?

Many salespeople become so good at selling excuses to themselves and their leaders that it becomes a way of life. They appear to have forgotten they're there to sell properties, not excuses.

Times *are* tough. Now what are you going to do about it? Are you going to manufacture excuses to disguise mediocrity, or are you going to work out what you need to do to get results and work that plan? Will you focus or fold?

Every day someone has bought or sold a house in your area, so why wasn't it you? And what can you do today to ensure it *will* be you tomorrow?

Measure and improve

In any professional sport, teams and individuals compete first with themselves and then with their opposition.

Athletes know their personal best (PB). When they beat their PB, this new PB becomes the one to beat. They measure their performances relative to their PB.

A personal best is a measurement. All coaches and players know if you can measure something, you can improve it.

This is just as true in Sales as it is in sport. And just as great coaches and players measure their performance, so too do great salespeople.

The basic measurements are easy to find in the company records: listings, sales, dollar production. Monitoring these numbers will help you track your progress. But the numbers alone won't show you *how* to improve.

There are other important numbers and key ratios, including:

- prospecting calls to listing appointments
- listing appointments to listings obtained
- listings obtained to listings sold
- substantial price reduction (SPR) appointments to SPRs obtained
- buyer property inspections to sales started
- sales started to settled sales
- online client reviews obtained (very important).

Too often, salespeople fail to keep score in these areas. As a result, they don't have performance statistics that could lead to massive improvement.

(Every industry has statistics. If you are not a real estate salesperson, seek out statistics that help you to calculate your goals, targets and plans. How many people do you need to speak with in order to get a good appointment? How many appointments lead to a sale? Always plan using accurate statistics as your guide.)

When you measure these numbers and ratios, you will soon see where you need to improve. For example, if you have a low appointment to listings ratio, that tells you two things: Your appointments were poorly qualified (you shouldn't have attended some — or all — of them in the first place), or your listing presentation needs work. You now know what you need to work on: qualifying, presenting or both.

Ratios tell you how much activity is required to produce a given result at your present skill level. A skilled telephone prospector, for example, might find one listing after 60 calls, whereas a person of lesser skill might need to make 120 calls to get a listing. These two ratios of 60:1 and 120:1 mean the person with lower skill will have to make twice as many calls to get the same result as the person with higher skill.

This isn't necessarily bad news. Even if you have lower skill, you can still get the same results as a person with higher skill if you are prepared to make the extra calls. More importantly, you can improve your skill and gradually lower the number of calls you need to make to get a result.

If you don't measure and know your ratios, you won't be able to measure the improvement, nor will you know why you are performing poorly. Without the statistics, you are flying blind.

The reliability of ratios can sometimes astound you. I once saw a person who had a 100:1 call to appointment ratio (100 calls got him one listing appointment) reach 99 calls and say, 'The next call gets me a listing appointment!' He was right: he listed that property. Of course, it was partly coincidence, but it was also confidence in his ability based on the numbers.

For many years, I have been talking with salespeople about the importance of measuring performance. Winners and potential winners are happy to gather the statistics, even if at first they don't know how to read them.

If you are going to work in Sales, you may as well become good at it. Measure your performance so you know what to improve.

Go on, take the blindfold off.

Summary

Competent action separates those who succeed from those who don't. It's the main reason why winners win and others don't. Some people have a great attitude, have the right knowledge and even have all the skills — but they don't take action.

What's next?

We have now completed the four-step process on our success journey: attitude, knowledge, skill and competent action.

However, you haven't completed your journey yet. These four steps can lead to success in your work, but they don't guarantee success in life. They can make you look like a winner in business, but real winners are winners in life as well. And for that we need one more thing: prosperity.

PART III

WINNING FOR LIFE

· ·

8

PROSPERITY

Both my wife and I grew up in families without much money. Kez often says, 'Even though I can afford it, sometimes I still have to convince myself it's okay to spend money on myself. I have to allow myself to deserve it.'

She once bought some towels for our bathroom but said, 'I'm not really happy with those towels.' I asked why she had bought them. 'Well, you know, the other ones were so expensive!' To which I replied, 'So you buy things you're not happy with?'

We have to allow ourselves to deserve prosperity. It's a lesson I had to learn myself.

I changed when I started setting goals, making plans and using affirmations. Things started to change for me when I wrote affirmations like this, 15 times a day for 21 days:

'I, Gary Pittard, accept and enjoy that I have received *[insert production result]* in *[month and year]*, and everything I do contributes to this result.'

I started to believe in myself. When I changed my thinking, I changed my actions. And when I did that, the belief manifested. I'll always thank Bill Nasby for showing me this path.

I mentioned earlier the importance of allowing ourselves to buy quality items. I once worked with a salesperson who was struggling financially, to the point where he only had one suit, which had a torn crotch. He used to go to listing presentations and cross his legs so people couldn't see the tear. Assuming he was presenting against an opponent with the same level of skill, who do you think got more listings—the one who felt like a winner or the one who was worried about uncrossing his legs because of the tear in his trousers? Remember, if the person isn't right, the results will never be right either.

Now I allow myself to enjoy some of the good things that are rewards for the work we do, and I see Kez teaching herself to do the same.

I spoke with a longstanding friend and client about his overseas holiday to see his daughter. He was worried about the expense and said to me, 'I probably shouldn't be doing it now, but we can afford it.' I said, 'Do you remember 20 years ago, when we talked about delayed gratification? I think now you're in your fifties, it's time for a bit of gratification. Don't delay now.'

There comes a time when all that delayed gratification must be rewarded. When that time comes, allow yourself to enjoy it, be grateful, and share it.

What's the point?

We have already covered the four steps on the journey to success:

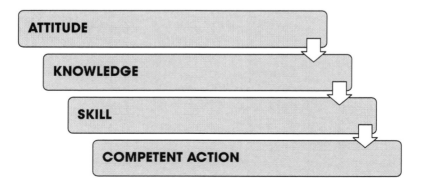

These steps will bring you success in business, but there's one more step for success in life: a prosperity mindset.

Prosperity isn't luck; just like everything else, it's a skill. It's about thinking abundance rather than scarcity, saving rather than splurging, building wealth rather than just earning money, giving back rather than always taking, and associating with the people who matter most to you.

Ultimately it's about happiness.

As Dr Denis Waitley says:

> *Happiness is the natural experience of winning your own self-respect, as well as the respect of others. Happiness should not be confused with indulgence, escapism, or hedonistic pleasure-seeking. You can't drink, inhale, or snort happiness. You can't buy it, wear it, drive it, swallow it, inject it, or travel to it! Happiness is the journey, not the destination. As elusive as a butterfly, happiness comes only to those who feel it without chasing it.*

In this chapter, we'll look at the things that create happiness and true prosperity.

Think abundance

Life offers us choice, so choose wisely. We can choose to be happy or sad. Spend too long being sad and it becomes a habit, and you can become a toxic person.

I know people who can't wait to get upset—even outraged—about something. They seldom say anything positive about anyone. Their arrogance is amazing: In their view, everyone else is stupid. They're always the victims. Everybody, it seems, is out to get them. When they use social media, it's primarily to denigrate other people. No doubt you know the type. Personally, I get them out of my life as quickly as possible.

Life is good—but you have to look for the good in life. If you look for bad things, you will probably find them. This can also become a habit and make you miserable. You can be optimistic without being blindly optimistic.

You can choose to be a 'glass half full' type of person or a 'glass half empty' type. I love focusing on abundance these days, but I had to practise to get to this point. What you focus on expands. Focus on abundance and you enjoy more abundance.

Be grateful

Do you know people who never stop complaining about the state of the country, the health system, the cost of living? Recognise how good your standard of living is, compared with many other parts of the world — perhaps even compared with many other people in your community.

With so much to choose from in life, be careful what you choose. Choose to be happy, to work hard on the right actions, to take good meaningful breaks, to focus on abundance, and to be grateful for your career, family and life.

Happiness is a choice and it comes from a good attitude and choosing wisely. Enjoy life and be grateful for what you have. The alternative looks pretty grim to me!

Save more

A friend once asked me, 'If your income dropped by 10 per cent, would you go broke? Could you afford to feed your family, and would you be able to pay the mortgage?' I replied, 'Yes, I could probably survive a 10 per cent drop.' To which he replied, 'Then why don't you save that 10 per cent?'

Not saving is just an excuse, just as not prospecting is an excuse.

I knew a couple who had retired and were visiting Sydney on a holiday. I offered to take them back to their accommodation—and discovered it was a backpackers' hostel not far from where I lived. They were in their seventies, staying in a backpackers' hostel. There's nothing wrong with hostels, of course, but I remembered thinking that I didn't want to be in my seventies and staying in a hostel because I couldn't afford anything else.

People seldom get rich quickly, so treat your money with respect. Most things in life are easier if you have money. Money should never be a goal in itself, but a reward for doing the right actions consistently over time. Money is a reward for competence, service and providing value.

If you're not getting results, you're currently incompetent. You can do something about it, but you have to accept the fact that it's not the market that is causing your poor performance. It's either lack of action or incompetent action that is the culprit.

You might be making money, but you can still be one payday away from bankruptcy. Winners develop the saving habit. When I got into that habit, things changed because I became a better salesperson—I could now talk *empathetically* to clients. I respected that they had saved up a large sum of money to buy their home. I could empathise with them because I had been through the same thing.

I hear some salespeople advise their clients to drop the price by $20000 as though it's nothing. This is irresponsible and shows a lack of respect for money, and for the clients and their situation. To the clients it is a lot of money—and it should be for you too. Try to save $20000 and tell me if it's not a lot of money! Treat money with respect. I'm not saying you should love money, but respect it. Once you have saved $20000 yourself, you'll develop a new respect for money.

Ben Stein says: 'Remind yourself life goes by with stunning breathtaking speed and you'll want to prepare for the day when you no longer have the strength to work or at least work as hard as you did when you were young and such preparation primarily takes the form of saving.'

Spending is not a substitute for saving. Many people use the term 'retail therapy' to justify buying themselves a better life by overspending on their credit cards. They have a cupboard full of shoes, most of which they've never worn, or they have a car bought during an ego-filled moment. When they try to sell the car to end the payments, it's worth only half of what they owe on it. This kind of spending can cost you dearly.

Develop a respect for money and save as much as you can. Buying with borrowed money will add to your debt, so don't borrow for anything that goes down in value (most credit card debt) and choose your investments carefully. Debt weighs people down with constant worry and anxiety, and eventually causes health problems. So learn to save.

Build wealth

My wife and I do not live an extravagant lifestyle. We've been in the same home for more than 20 years, have secure investments and spend time with our family at our holiday home. We travel when it suits us, which is not every year.

Wealth and prosperity come from saving, careful investments and an understanding that there is no such thing as a 'get rich quick' scheme. Be patient. Accumulate wealth and become prosperous over time. There's nothing wrong with wanting to be rich, but I don't want to be obscenely rich. I want enough money so I don't have money worries now, and so Kez won't have any money worries if I die before her. I also want to make sure our children and grandchildren are financially secure.

If you insure your income, you will be paid 75 per cent of your income if accident or illness prevents you from working. Insure your life, property and investments. You can insure many things, but you can't insure against living too long. Make sure that, however long you live, you live in a manner of your choosing, not some politician's whim about whether you're going to get an extra $20 a fortnight on your pension.

I was told a story of a Holocaust survivor who came to Australia and prospered. In his old age, he suffered a series of strokes. The doctors wanted to put him into a care facility where he could be looked after, but he didn't want to go. He lived in a two-storey house, so he installed an inclinator for his wheelchair. Now that he could get up and down the stairs, he was able to live—and eventually die—in the house he loved, surrounded by his loved ones.

He said being old is one thing, being old and sick is worse, but worst of all would be to be old, sick and broke. I have never forgotten that story.

Give back

No-one succeeds alone. People will help you along the way, so be sure to give back. Your willingness to help others and to share your success come from the winning quality of gratitude.

Be grateful for what you have and to the people who have helped you along the way. It makes the success journey more fulfilling.

Help people with no expectation of a reward.

I've been blessed with people in my life who have given me time, expertise and knowledge. People are givers and the world cannot survive without people giving back. When you give back, you feel more grateful for your success.

Giving is an attitude. What would the world be like if everyone took but didn't give back?

If we're going to share this planet, we have to contribute. As people contributed to your success, you must contribute to theirs and to the success of others.

Associate with the right people

Parents want the best for their children. One way they show this is to pay attention to the people their children mix with. It isn't difficult to identify the undesirable type of child: They are rough kids—often impolite, angry and bad-mannered. These 'bad' boys and girls appeal to others because of their wild side, but if you allow your children to mix with them for too long, trouble is certain. You might not always identify them immediately, but eventually their bad behaviour becomes obvious.

Parents often have one rule for their children and another for themselves. They tell their children to avoid drugs, while they drink a beer. They smack their children for hitting other children, yet all they really teach their children is that you can get away with these things if you are bigger. Mixed messages abound.

You don't want your children mixing with the wrong type of person. But what about *you*? Are you as particular about the people you spend time with? The wrong people drag you down; the right people make life better.

Be mindful of the people with whom you spend time.

Clients

Select only those clients you feel are reasonable, approachable people. They might become lifelong clients. If you are an active prospector, you have more choice of clients than desperate salespeople who don't spend much time looking for new business.

Don't deal with people who don't trust agents, who feel they know more than you do, who don't show respect, who don't give you a fair hearing or who 'shoot the messenger' whenever you deliver bad news. Leave these clients to desperate salespeople. Seek a higher quality client.

Friends

Your friends influence you, for good or bad. Charlie 'Tremendous' Jones says: 'You will be the same person in five years as you are today except for the people you meet and the books you read.'

Think about your so-called friends. Do you have any who emotionally drain you, who complain about their lives, find fault with you and your life, complain about the government, their job, their boss—everything? Do you feel uplifted after spending time with this person? No? Then why are you wasting your life on people like that?

Perhaps you are co-dependent and think you can change them, but you will never raise them to your level. They will drag you down to theirs instead.

I know a man who, every time we meet, takes it upon himself to give me advice about how I conduct my life. He tells me I work too hard. 'It's not all about money, you know!', he says, before reeling off just about every other balanced-life cliché you know.

But I have a family I'm proud of, a great business, and so much more to be grateful for. I live with people I love living with and do work I love doing. I work with people I love working with, and we are financially sound. We are content.

Now for my 'friend': He's nearly fifty, single and has never been in a long-term relationship. He is also broke, lazy and complains about how little money he has. He jams his advice down my throat because he feels that if he can find fault with my life, it will make his miserable life look a bit brighter.

My solution: I don't see him, unless by accident. I bump into him from time to time, but keep the conversation at a superficial level. I don't need or want his advice, because I don't want to be like him.

Real friends want you to be happy and successful. They're happy when you are happy. They aren't jealous of your success or resentful of it. If they think you are going down the wrong path, they will tell you, but with the highest of motives: your wellbeing.

Run a broom through your figurative Friend Closet from time to time. Get rid of downers, toxics and trolls.

Family

Who says you have to like every member of your family? You don't! A controversial thought, I know, but if you have a family member who is similar to the 'friend' I mentioned, spend as little time with this person as you can. If he gets drunk at a family function and targets you, don't smile politely; call him on his bad behaviour.

In *Pulling Your Own Strings*, Dr Wayne Dyer will teach you how to set boundaries for badly behaved people and how to eliminate their power to bully, manipulate and belittle you.

Some family members you see out of love, others out of perceived duty. You teach people how to treat you. If you leave family functions feeling angry, frustrated or resentful, why go back for more of the same treatment? Because you have to? You don't.

These days, I don't care whether it is clients, friends or family, I do my best to spend as much time with the right people and to reduce, or eliminate completely, encounters with the wrong ones.

The right people make life better. Mix with the right people, in all areas of your life.

Summary

It is easy to ignore, neglect or defer prosperity, to think you can do it later 'when I have the time' or 'when I can afford it'. But prosperity is worth working toward, sooner rather than later. Develop a prosperity mindset.

9

WINNERS ARE DOERS

Over the years, I have seen many seminar junkies who use seminar attendance as a way of forestalling action. These people never succeed.

Others seek out winners and ask for their advice, but never do anything with that advice. These people fare no better than the seminar junkies. They want to talk about success instead of actually doing something about it.

Winners win because they learn what they need to do to be successful, and then they do it. For winners, life is an action fest, not a talk fest. Winners are doers.

Jack Collis advises, 'Be positive, believe in yourself, trust your intuition, be decisive and get on with it.' As the Persian proverb goes, 'Not everyone who chased something ever caught it, but those who caught it had chased it.' Have a go!

When Shannon Goodson was asked for her definition of a sales professional, she said, 'A truly professional salesperson is an individual who has the ability and emotional discipline necessary to make cold calls when they're necessary but who has been trained so well they never have to.'

I agree with most of this, though not with the word 'never'. In the early years of our careers, we must build a pipeline of referral business, and this takes time. It begins with cold calling strangers, then following them up over the medium to long term, turning strangers into clients, then into referral business. Through cold calling we meet strangers; through consistent follow-up we turn strangers into clients, and then into what I call 'easy business'—referred business.

Make the cold calls but add potential clients to your contact list daily. Follow up regularly and eventually you'll start working with people you have had contact with in the past. You make more warm calls, but if you have to, you know exactly how to prospect for new business because you've done it in the past. That is what I think Goodson means in her definition of success.

Some people have never paid their dues, so of course they're not going to get the rewards. It's like hosing concrete and expecting corn to grow. You can't expect a result without putting in the work.

Over the years I have heard mediocre salespeople refer to winners as 'freaks'. But my observation of winners is different. Winners define what success means to them and then work towards it. What actions would you do if you were the best salesperson in the world?

If I was the best salesperson in the world:

- *I would set goals.* I know that to focus for the long term, I have to work toward something worthwhile. Goals give me focus.

- *I would plan.* Mediocre people drift through their days, weeks, months and years. They're unfocused and have no direction. These people often say, 'I can't believe we're almost at the end of the year!' Did they plan their poor performance, or was poor performance the result of failing to plan?

- *I would write daily affirmations.* I know that whenever I want to take my performance to a higher level, I must believe I can do it—even more, I must feel as though I am *already doing it.* Affirmations make me feel as though I have already achieved my desired success level. I am more likely to act in accordance with what I believe.

- *I would work hard.* I would work hard on the right actions by following my clear plan every day.

- *I would keep my promises.* I would start with promises I make to myself. If I say I am going to do something, I do it. If, for example, I promise myself to speak with 40 potential clients each day, I keep that promise, as I do all promises I make.

- *I would spend every working morning searching for new business.* My desired success level requires me to make more sales. This means I need more stock to sell. Losers sit and wait for business to walk through the door. I don't.

- *I would study.* I know if I devote an hour a day to studying my craft, it will help me to accomplish more in less time.

- *I would practise what I learn.* From study comes knowledge, but from practice comes skill. I need skill to turn leads into listings, then into sales, and then into happy clients.

- *I would guard my time.* People don't steal my time. I choose to give it away or not. I choose to give my time to people who want to buy my product or service, or who may need my help to get into a position to do so. Clients who deal with me treat me with the same level of courtesy and respect as I do them.

- *I would try to do what is right in all situations.* To put money ahead of doing what is right chips away at my integrity. I never choose short-term gain at the expense of my reputation. My good name is my brand.

- *I would work with my sellers* to help them understand the market. I do this gently and with understanding and honest advice, never resorting to conditioning and pressure tactics. This doesn't mean I will be soft, though. If a client's property is overpriced for the current market, I am honour-bound to point this out.

- *I would work with my buyers* to help them buy the right property under the right terms. This doesn't mean helping them to get the property at a *low* price, but it does mean ensuring the transaction is fair, with no information withheld.

- *I would take pride in my team and my company.* Even if I don't own it, I will always represent my company with enthusiasm and never commit it to anything that will cause it to lose profit. Giveaways are poor substitutes for skill. I never resort to discounting my fee or giving 'freebies' to win business.

- *I would ask questions.* I may make the occasional assumption, but I always take the time to test those assumptions before making recommendations. To make recommendations without first knowing what clients need, and to a lesser degree what they want, is irresponsible. I make informed recommendations because I am a professional.

- *I would close.* I will ask for the business at every presentation. I will ask more than once — five times or more. I will ask buyers to buy and sellers to list with me.

- *I would allow plenty of family time.* True success is a complete package. How sad to be wealthy but to have your family despise you. I don't call that success. My family is the bedrock of any success I enjoy. They will never take second place.

And above all...

- *I would turn 'I would' into 'I do'.* If I want to *become* the best salesperson in the world, I must change 'I would' to 'I do'. One is a statement of intent, the other is action.

Jim Stovall says this in *The Ultimate Gift*: 'In the end, a person is only known by the impact they have on others.'

We have a great opportunity to make a positive impact on many people. Home sellers look for good agents who care and who will get them the highest possible prices for their properties. Home buyers also need someone who can help them by guiding them and treating them fairly.

You have a great chance to make positive impacts on your family, your friends and the people you meet. You have a chance to share the success you enjoy from the life you have built for yourself. Sales is a wonderful career.

Decide what must be done, and do it. Every day.

This is the success journey winners follow.

And then, one day, someone may just call *you* the best salesperson in the world.

Someone has to hold that title. Why not you?

INDEX

Connect *with* WILEY ▶▶▶

WILEY

Browse and purchase the full range of Wiley publications on our official website.

www.wiley.com

Check out the Wiley blog for news, articles and information from Wiley and our authors.

www.wileybizaus.com

Join the conversation on Twitter and keep up to date on the latest news and events in business.

@WileyBizAus

Sign up for Wiley newsletters to learn about our latest publications, upcoming events and conferences, and discounts available to our customers.

www.wiley.com/email

Wiley titles are also produced in e-book formats. Available from all good retailers.

WILEY

Learn more with practical advice from our experts

Smart Work
Dermot Crowley

Brave
Margie Warrell

Hooked
Gabrielle Dolan

Power Play
Yamini Naidu

The Ultimate Book of Influence
Chris Helder

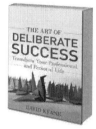

The Art of Deliberate Success
David Keane

The Four Mindsets
Anna-Lucia Mackay

The Naked CEO
Alex Malley

Useful Belief
Chris Helder